ADORABLE MINI DOLLS

by MOMO-TARO

CONTENTS

★ Copyright © 1988 ONDORISHA PUBLISHERS, LTD. All rights reserved.
★ Published by ONDORISHA PUBLISHERS, LTD., 32 Nishigoken-cho, Shinjuku-ku, Tokyo 162, Japan.
★ Sole Overseas Distributor: Japan Publications Trading Co., Ltd.
  P.O. Box 5030 Tokyo International, Tokyo, Japan.
★ Distributed in the United States by Kodansha International/USA, Ltd.
  114 Fifth Avenue, New York, NY 10011.
  Australia by Bookwise International, 54 Crittenden Road, Findon, South Australia 5007, Australia

10 9 8 7 6 5 4 3 2

ISBN 0-87040-761-9
Printed in Japan

LESSON 1

Shown on pgs. 8-9

	Felt	Broadcloth	Others
Donkey	20cm(8") square brown. 8cm(3¼") square flesh. 6cm(2½") square dark brown. Scraps of deep pink.	Scraps of black and gray	Fiberfill, Cement glue, Orange marker
Rabbit	15×20cm(6"×8") pink. 6cm(2½") square light pink. Scraps of flesh and deep pink.	Scraps of black	13cm (5¼") cotton string, Cement glue, Fiberfill, Orange marker.
Goose	10×15cm (4"×6") white. 5cm (2") square orange.	Scraps of black	Fiberfill, Orange marker, Cement glue.
Squirrel	10×15cm (4"×6") gold. Scraps of dark brown.	Scraps of black	Brown felt pen, Cement glue, Fiberfill, Orange marker

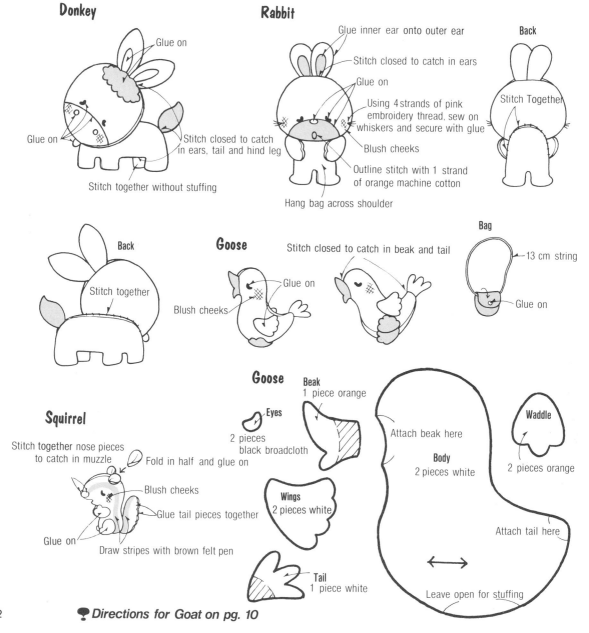

🌷 **Directions for Goat on pg. 10**

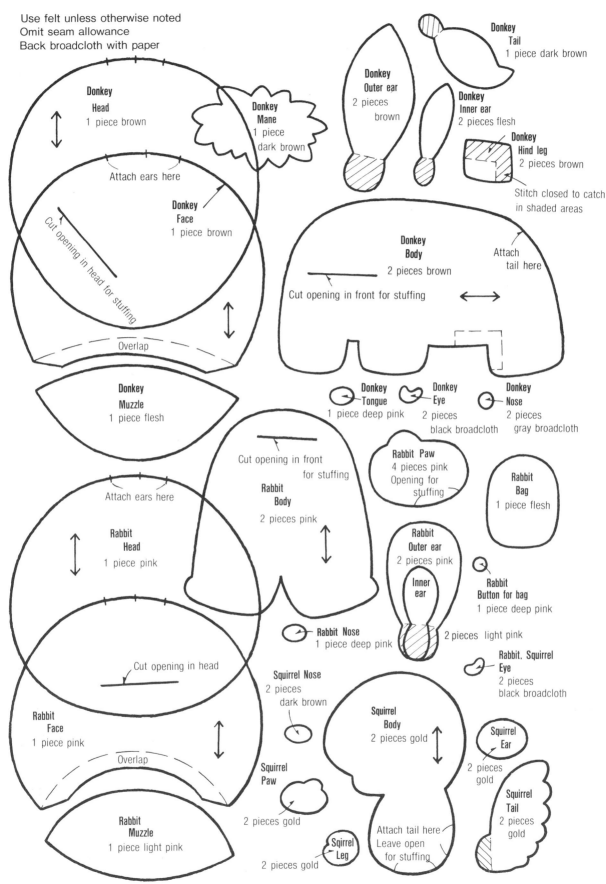

Use felt unless otherwise noted
Omit seam allowance
Back broadcloth with paper

Donkey
Tail
1 piece dark brown

Donkey
Outer ear
2 pieces
brown

Donkey
Inner ear
2 pieces flesh

Donkey
Head
1 piece brown

Donkey
Mane
1 piece
dark brown

Donkey
Hind leg
2 pieces brown

Stitch closed to catch
in shaded areas

Attach ears here

Donkey
Face
1 piece brown

Cut opening in head for stuffing

Donkey
Body
2 pieces brown

Attach
tail here

Cut opening in front for stuffing

Overlap

Donkey
Muzzle
1 piece flesh

Donkey
Tongue
1 piece deep pink

Donkey
Eye
2 pieces
black broadcloth

Donkey
Nose
2 pieces
gray broadcloth

Cut opening in front
for stuffing

Rabbit
Body
2 pieces pink

Rabbit Paw
4 pieces pink
Opening for
stuffing

Rabbit
Bag
1 piece flesh

Attach ears here

Rabbit
Head
1 piece pink

Rabbit
Outer ear
2 pieces pink

Inner
ear

Rabbit
Button for bag
1 piece deep pink

Cut opening in head

Rabbit Nose
1 piece deep pink

2 pieces light pink

Rabbit, Squirrel
Eye
2 pieces
black broadcloth

Rabbit
Face
1 piece pink

Squirrel Nose
2 pieces
dark brown

Squirrel
Body
2 pieces gold

Squirrel
Ear
2 pieces
gold

Overlap

Squirrel
Paw

Squirrel
Tail
2 pieces
gold

2 pieces gold

Rabbit
Muzzle
1 piece light pink

Sqirrel
Leg
2 pieces gold

Attach tail here
Leave open
for stuffing

3

4

Choo Choo Train

Choo Choo Train

Shown on pgs. 4-5

	Felt	Broadcloth	Others	Common Materials
Bear	20cm(8") square beige. 5×10cm(2"×4") dark gray. Scraps of black, flesh and deep pink.	Scraps of black and white		Fiberfill White paint Orange marker Cement glue
Dog	20cm(8") square white. 6×5cm(2½"×2") gray. Scraps of beige.	Scraps of black and white		
Mouse	10×12cm(4"×4¾") pink. Scraps of deep pink.	Scraps of black	White embroidery thread	
Giraffe	15×20cm(6"×8") bright yellow. 8cm(3¼") square brown. 1×15cm(⅜"×6") light green. Scraps of orange and white.	Scraps of black and white		

Bear

① Head, Body

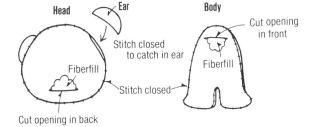

②

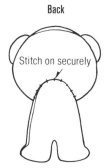

Back

③ Hat

Sew on hat

Glue on

Blush cheeks with marker

Eye

White paint

Glue together

Glue on

Dog

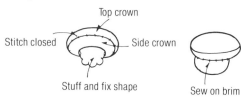

Glue on

Fold in half and catch in when closing

Blush cheeks with marker

White paint

Mouse

Glue on

Fold in ears

Back

Blush cheeks

Using 4 strands of white embroidery thread, sew on whiskers and secure with glue

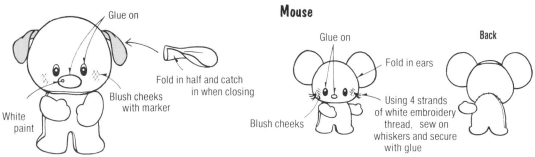

🍷 *Directions for Giraffe on pg. 75*

Use felt unless otherwise noted
Back broadcloth with paper
Omit seam allowance

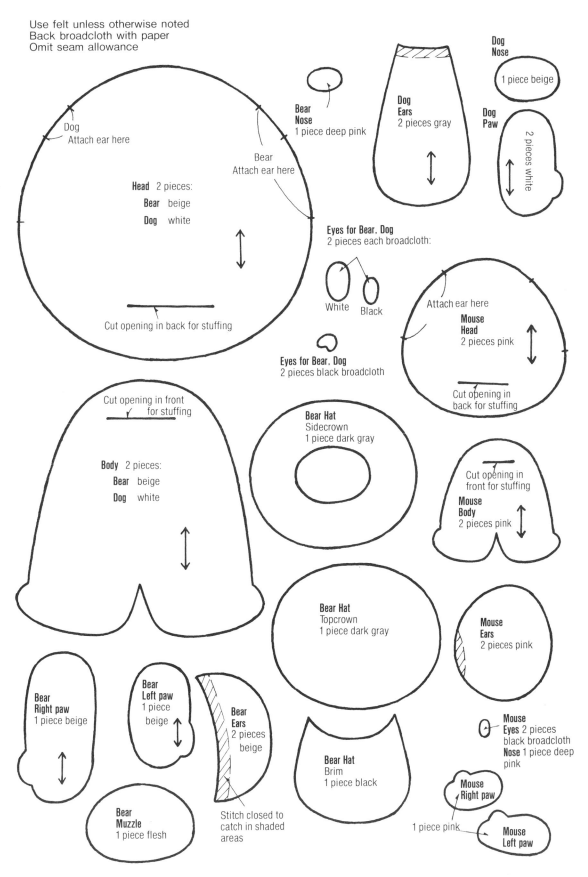

Dog
Attach ear here

Bear
Attach ear here

Bear
Nose
1 piece deep pink

Dog
Ears
2 pieces gray

Dog
Nose
1 piece beige

Dog
Paw
2 pieces white

Head 2 pieces:
Bear beige
Dog white

Eyes for Bear, Dog
2 pieces each broadcloth:

White Black

Attach ear here

Mouse
Head
2 pieces pink

Cut opening in back for stuffing

Eyes for Bear, Dog
2 pieces black broadcloth

Cut opening in
back for stuffing

Cut opening in front
for stuffing

Body 2 pieces:
Bear beige
Dog white

Bear Hat
Sidecrown
1 piece dark gray

Cut opening in
front for stuffing

Mouse
Body
2 pieces pink

Bear
Right paw
1 piece beige

Bear
Left paw
1 piece
beige

Bear
Ears
2 pieces
beige

Bear Hat
Topcrown
1 piece dark gray

Mouse
Ears
2 pieces pink

Bear Hat
Brim
1 piece black

Mouse
Eyes 2 pieces
black broadcloth
Nose 1 piece deep
pink

Bear
Muzzle
1 piece flesh

Stitch closed to
catch in shaded
areas

Mouse
Right paw

1 piece pink

Mouse
Left paw

7

Lesson 1

LESSON 1

Shown on pgs. 8-9

	Felt	Broadcloth	Others
Goat	20cm(8") square light brown. 15×20cm(6"×8") each gray, dark brown. 5×10cm(2"×4") each white, black. Scraps of beige and orange.	Scraps of black	Brown, Orange machine cotton. Scraps of gold acetate. Thin gold chain of 16cm(6¼") White paint. #20 white paper-wrapped wire. Fiberfill. Orange marker. Cement glue.

Goat

① **Body**

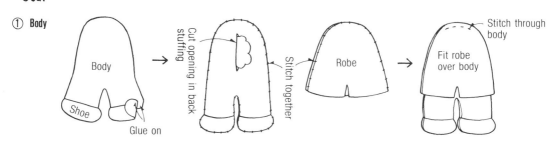

② **Face**

Stitch closed to catch in horns and ears

Stuffing

Fold in half

Cut opening in back

③

Back

Attach head slightly cocked

Stitch firmly together

④ **Sleeve, front leg**

Stitch through front leg

Stitch sides

Stuffing

Fit sleeve over front leg

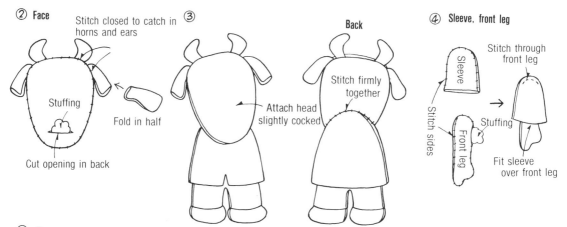

⑤ **Glasses**

White paper-wrapped wire 3cm (1¼")

⑥ **Cross**

16cm (6¼") chain

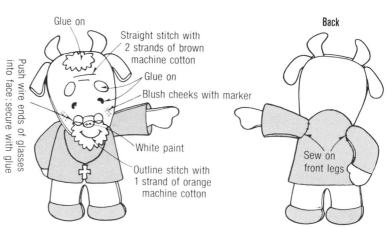

Glue on

Straight stitch with 2 strands of brown machine cotton

Glue on

Blush cheeks with marker

Push wire ends of glasses into face; secure with glue

White paint

Outline stitch with 1 strand of orange machine cotton

Back

Sew on front legs

🏵 *Directions for Donkey, Rabbit, Goose, and Squirrel on pg. 2*

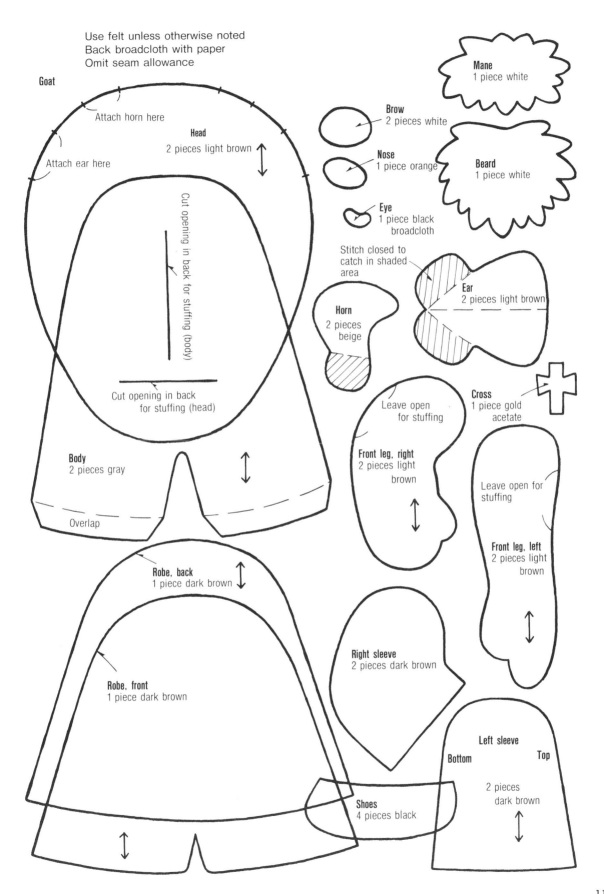

Use felt unless otherwise noted
Back broadcloth with paper
Omit seam allowance

Goat

Attach horn here

Head
2 pieces light brown

Attach ear here

Cut opening in back for stuffing (body)

Cut opening in back
for stuffing (head)

Body
2 pieces gray

Overlap

Mane
1 piece white

Brow
2 pieces white

Nose
1 piece orange

Beard
1 piece white

Eye
1 piece black
broadcloth

Stitch closed to
catch in shaded
area

Ear
2 pieces light brown

Horn
2 pieces
beige

Cross
1 piece gold
acetate

Leave open
for stuffing

Front leg, right
2 pieces light
brown

Leave open for
stuffing

Front leg, left
2 pieces light
brown

Robe, back
1 piece dark brown

Robe, front
1 piece dark brown

Right sleeve
2 pieces dark brown

Left sleeve

Bottom   Top

2 pieces
dark brown

Shoes
4 pieces black

11

Little Farmers

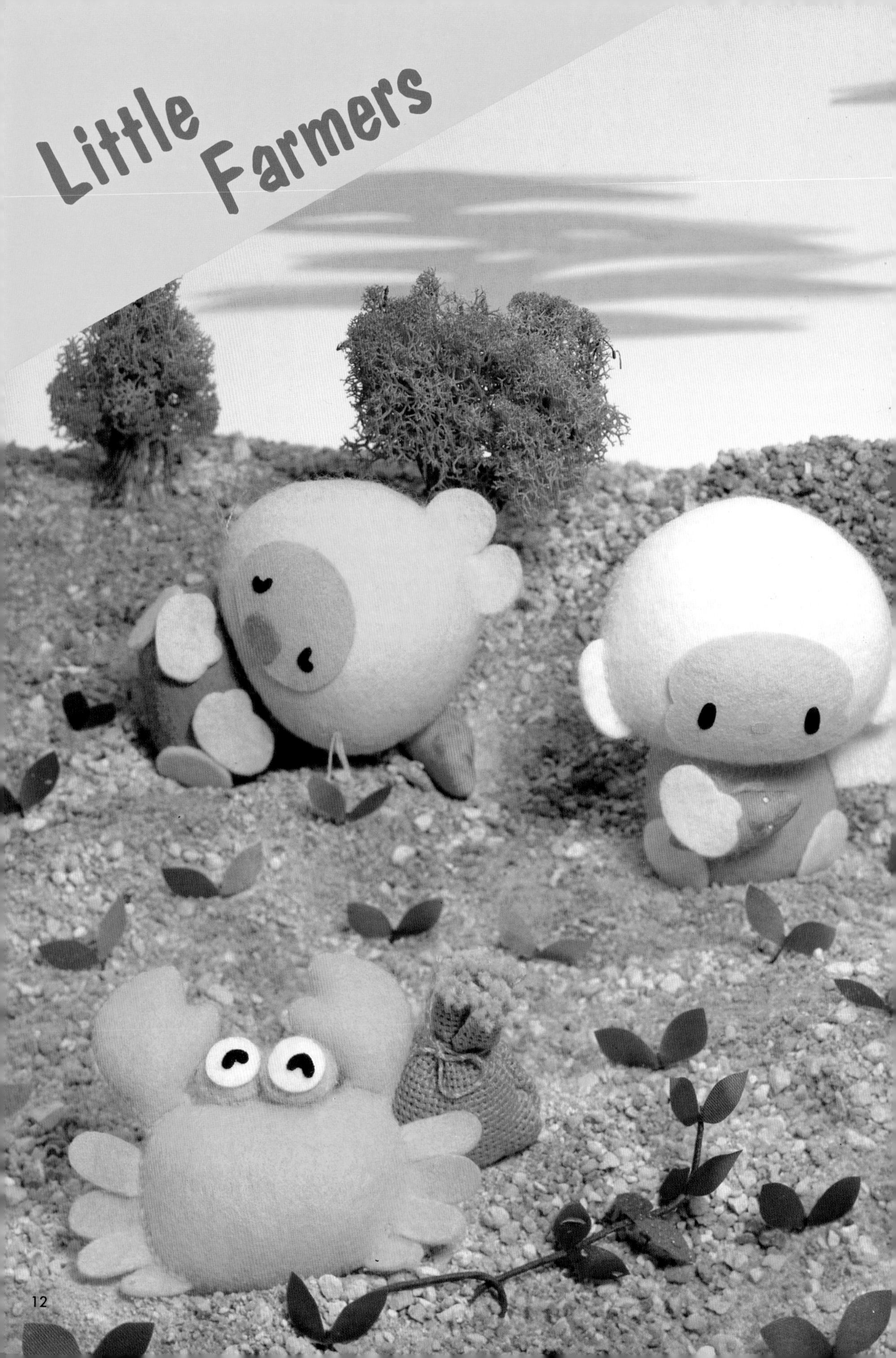

LITTLE FARMERS

Shown on pgs. 12-13

	Felt	Broadcloth	Others	Common Materials
Monkey	18×10cm(7"×4") white. 5×4cm(2"×1½") flesh. 12×6cm(5"×2½") pale purple.	Scraps of black, salmon pink.		Fiberfill Cement glue Orange marker (excluded for crab and snail)
Racoon	18×10cm(7"×4") flesh. 12×6cm(5"×2½") blue. Scraps of orange and brick red.	Scraps of black.	Flesh-color embroidery thread.	
Tiger	18×10cm(7"×4") pale yellow. 12×6cm(5"×2½") light green. Scraps of white and orange.	Scraps of black.	Ivory embroidery thread, Brown felt pen.	
Elephant	20cm(8") square beige. 17×8cm(7"×3¼") brown. Scraps of white.	Scraps of black.	#25 white paper-wrapped wire.	
Crab	15×12cm(6"×5") pink. Scraps of white.	Scraps of black.		
Snail	10cm(4") square each cream, mustard yellow. Scraps of white.	Scraps of black.	#25 white paper-wrapped wire. Brown embroidery thread.	
Mole	6cm(2½") square orange.		Black, brick red machine cotton.	

Common directions

① Head, Body

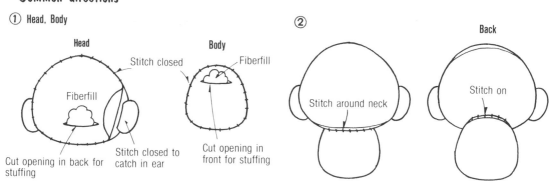

🍄 *Directions for Elephant, Crab, Snail and Mole on pg. 68*

Tiger

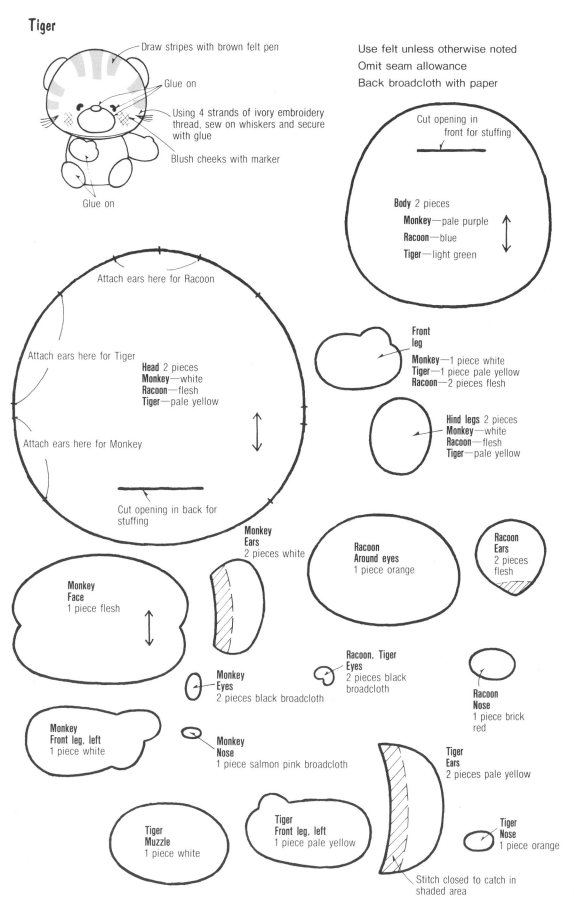

Draw stripes with brown felt pen

Glue on

Using 4 strands of ivory embroidery thread, sew on whiskers and secure with glue

Blush cheeks with marker

Glue on

Use felt unless otherwise noted
Omit seam allowance
Back broadcloth with paper

Cut opening in front for stuffing

Body 2 pieces
Monkey—pale purple
Racoon—blue
Tiger—light green

Attach ears here for Racoon

Attach ears here for Tiger

Head 2 pieces
Monkey—white
Racoon—flesh
Tiger—pale yellow

Attach ears here for Monkey

Cut opening in back for stuffing

Front leg
Monkey—1 piece white
Tiger—1 piece pale yellow
Racoon—2 pieces flesh

Hind legs 2 pieces
Monkey—white
Racoon—flesh
Tiger—pale yellow

Monkey Ears
2 pieces white

Racoon Around eyes
1 piece orange

Racoon Ears
2 pieces flesh

Monkey Face
1 piece flesh

Monkey Eyes
2 pieces black broadcloth

Racoon, Tiger Eyes
2 pieces black broadcloth

Racoon Nose
1 piece brick red

Monkey Front leg, left
1 piece white

Monkey Nose
1 piece salmon pink broadcloth

Tiger Ears
2 pieces pale yellow

Tiger Muzzle
1 piece white

Tiger Front leg, left
1 piece pale yellow

Tiger Nose
1 piece orange

Stitch closed to catch in shaded area

15

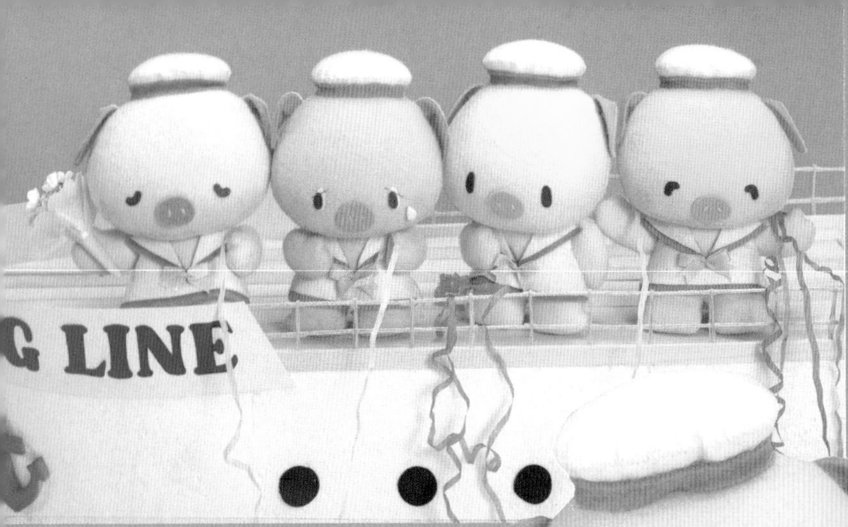
G LINE

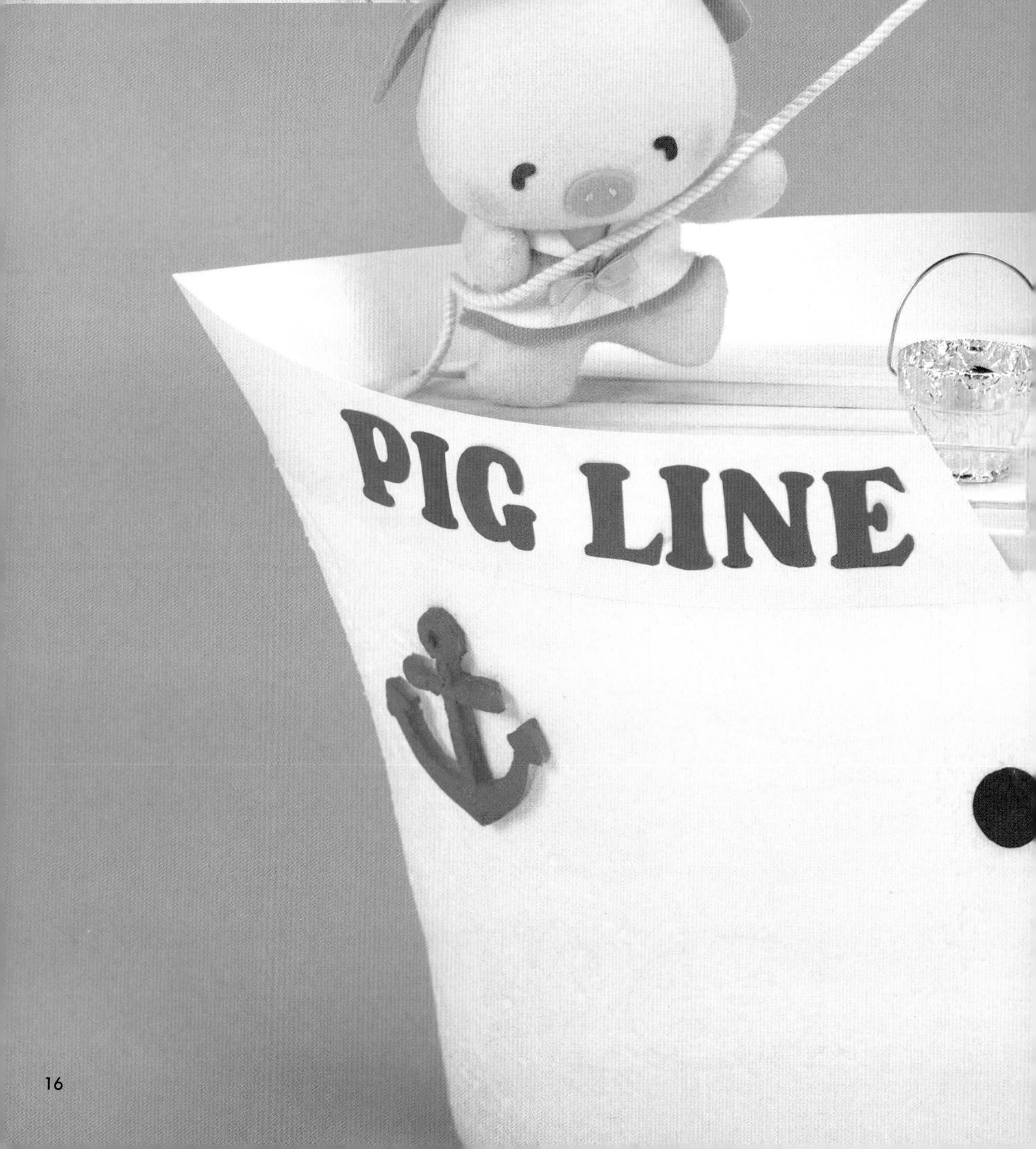
PIG LINE

Pig Sailors

PIG SAILORS

Shown on pgs. 16-17

		Felt	Broadcloth	Machine Cotton	Ribbon	Others (Common Materials)
A·E		20×25cm(8"×10") pale orange. 13×20cm (5¼"×8") white. 5×10cm(2"×4") orange. 4×15cm(1½"×6") purple.	Scraps of gray.	Yellow	Lavender	Fiberfill Cement glue Orange marker
B·G		20×25cm(8"×10") pink. 13×20cm(5¼"×8") white. 5×10cm(2"×4") deep pink. 4×15cm(1½"×6") purple.	Scraps of white and gray.	Pink Gray	Lavender (Not used for G)	
C·F		20×25cm(8"×10") cream. 13×20cm (5¼"×8") white. 5×10cm(2"×4") light green. 4×15cm(1½"×6") blue.	Scraps of gray.	Ivory	Light blue	
D		20×25cm(8"×10") flesh. 13×20cm(5¼"×8") white. 5×10cm(2"×4") beige. 4×15cm(1½"×6") blue.	Scraps of gray.	Ivory	Light blue	

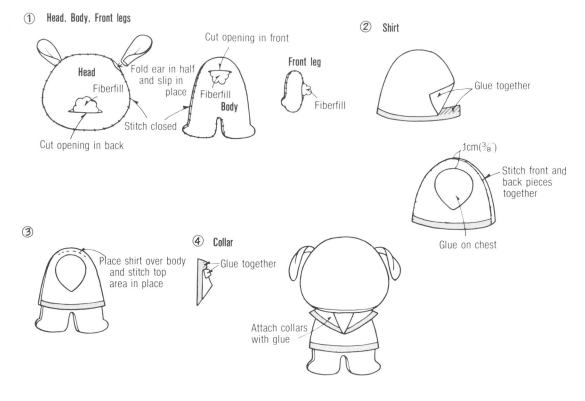

① Head, Body, Front legs

Head
Fiberfill
Cut opening in back
Fold ear in half and slip in place
Cut opening in front
Fiberfill
Stitch closed
Body
Front leg
Fiberfill

② Shirt

Glue together
1cm(⅜")
Stitch front and back pieces together
Glue on chest

③
Place shirt over body and stitch top area in place

④ Collar
Glue together
Attach collars with glue

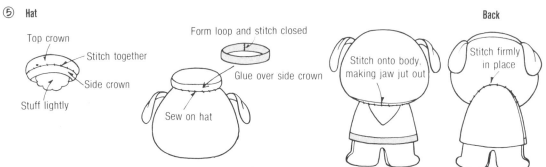

⑤ Hat

Top crown
Stitch together
Side crown
Stuff lightly
Form loop and stitch closed
Glue over side crown
Sew on hat

Back

Stitch onto body, making jaw jut out

Stitch firmly in place

A

Back

🍷 *Pattern on pg. 70*

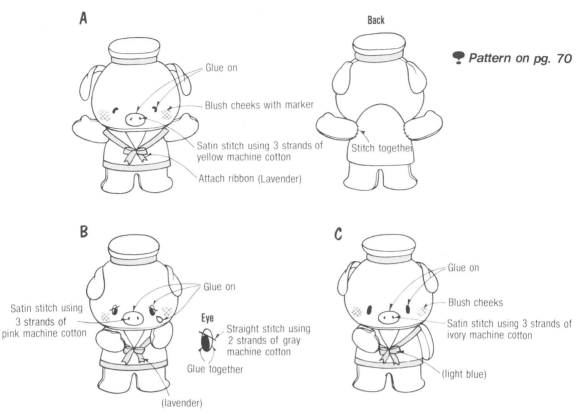

Glue on

Blush cheeks with marker

Satin stitch using 3 strands of
yellow machine cotton

Attach ribbon (Lavender)

Stitch together

B

Satin stitch using
3 strands of
pink machine cotton

Glue on

Eye

Straight stitch using
2 strands of gray
machine cotton

Glue together

(lavender)

C

Glue on

Blush cheeks

Satin stitch using 3 strands of
ivory machine cotton

(light blue)

D

Glue on

Blush cheeks

Satin stitch using
3 strands of ivory
machine cotton

(light blue)

F

Back

Glue on

Blush cheeks

Satin stitch using
3 strands of ivory
machine cotton

(light blue)

E

Glue on

Blush cheeks

Satin stitch using
3 strands of
yellow machine cotton

(lavender)

G

Back

Glue on

Blush cheeks

Satin stitch using
3 strands of
pink machine cotton

Attach line with glue

Stitch on

19

Ice Sports

ICE SPORTS

Shown on pgs. 20-21

	Felt	Broadcloth	Others	Common Materials
Penguin	10×20cm(4"×8") light green. 7×15cm(2¾"×6") white. 6cm(2½") square orange.	Scraps of black		Fiberfill Cement glue Orange marker (excluding whale)
Seal	15cm(6") square beige. 2×15cm(¾"×6") white. Scraps of dark brown.	Scraps of black, white	Black, Orange machine cotton. Brown felt pen. White paint.	
Turtle	6×11cm(2½"×4½") each lavender, purple, flesh. 2×10cm(¾"×4") white.	Scraps of black	White paint.	
Polar Bear	20cm(8") square white. Scraps of flesh color, deep pink.	Scraps of black	White paint.	
Whale	20×26cm(8"×10¼") blue. 10×15cm(4"×6") pale blue. 2×25cm(¾"×10") white.	Scraps of black	Orange machine cotton.	

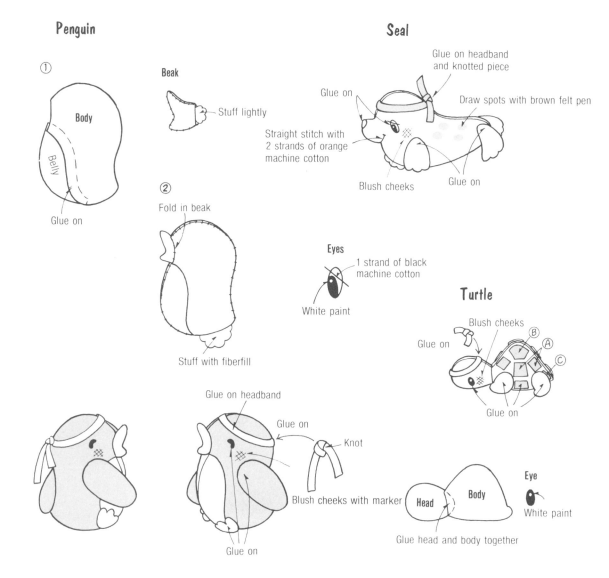

Penguin

① Body / Belly / Glue on

Beak — Stuff lightly

② Fold in beak / Stuff with fiberfill

Seal

Glue on headband and knotted piece

Glue on

Draw spots with brown felt pen

Straight stitch with 2 strands of orange machine cotton

Blush cheeks

Glue on

Eyes — 1 strand of black machine cotton / White paint

Turtle

Blush cheeks

Glue on

Ⓐ Ⓑ Ⓒ

Glue on

Head / Body / Glue head and body together

Eye — White paint

Glue on headband

Glue on

Knot

Blush cheeks with marker

Glue on

♥ *Directions for Polar Bear and Whale on pg. 72*

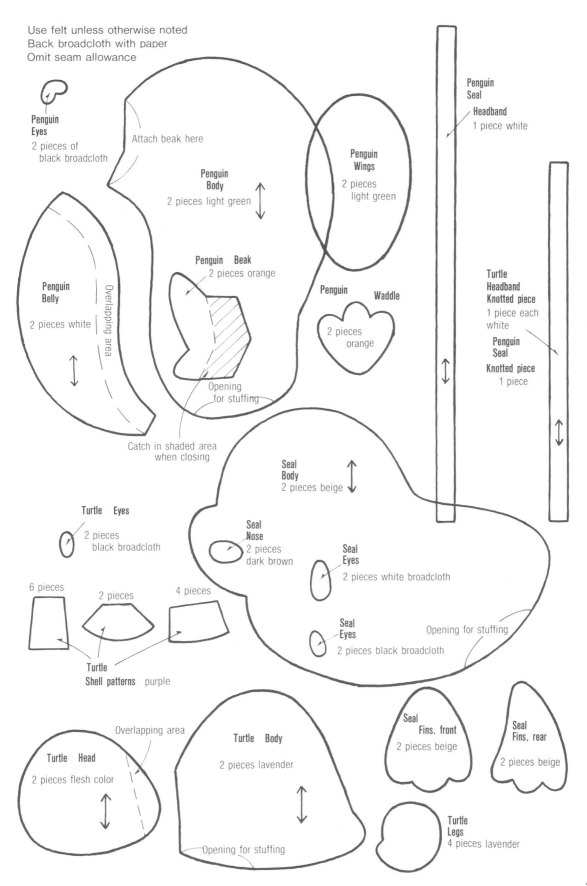

Use felt unless otherwise noted
Back broadcloth with paper
Omit seam allowance

Penguin
Eyes
2 pieces of
black broadcloth

Attach beak here

Penguin
Body
2 pieces light green

Penguin
Wings
2 pieces
light green

Penguin
Seal
Headband
1 piece white

Penguin   Beak
2 pieces orange

Penguin   Waddle
2 pieces
orange

Turtle
Headband
Knotted piece
1 piece each
white

Penguin
Seal
Knotted piece
1 piece

Penguin
Belly
2 pieces white

Overlapping area

Opening
for stuffing

Catch in shaded area
when closing

Seal
Body
2 pieces beige

Turtle   Eyes
2 pieces
black broadcloth

Seal
Nose
2 pieces
dark brown

Seal
Eyes
2 pieces white broadcloth

6 pieces

2 pieces

4 pieces

Seal
Eyes
2 pieces black broadcloth

Opening for stuffing

Turtle
Shell patterns   purple

Overlapping area

Turtle   Body
2 pieces lavender

Seal
Fins, front
2 pieces beige

Seal
Fins, rear
2 pieces beige

Turtle   Head
2 pieces flesh color

Opening for stuffing

Turtle
Legs
4 pieces lavender

23

ROCK CLIMBING

Shown on pgs. 24-25

	Felt	Broadcloth	Thread	Others
Racoon A · B	20cm(8") square flesh. 15×8cm(6"×3¼") blue. 6cm(2½") square beige. Scraps of dark brown.	Scraps of black, white (White not required for A).	Ivory embroidery thread. White paint.	Fiberfill(not used for camera). Cement glue. Orange marker (not used for backpack and camera). Black marker(for backpack only).
Fox A · B	20cm(8") square gold. 15×8cm(6"×3¼") olive green. Scraps of dark brown.	Scraps of black, white(for A only).	Gold embroidery thread. Black machine cotton (for B only).	
Crow	15×10cm(6"×4") black. 8cm(3¼") square deep pink.	Scraps of black, white.		
Camera	Scraps of white.	Scraps of black.	Black machine cotton.	
Backpack Large(Small)	10×14cm(4"×5½") brown(orange). Scraps of beige (pale orange).			

① Head, Body, Front and hind legs, Tail

② Back

③ Face

Ear — Fold in

Head

Fiberfill

Stitch closed

Cut opening in back for stuffing

Body

Fiberfill

Cut opening in front for stuffing

Stitch firmly

Front leg — Fiberfill
Hind leg — Fiberfill

Glue on

Tail — Tip of tail — Fiberfill

Racoon A

Back

Glue on

Using 6 strands of ivory embroidery thread, sew on whiskers and secure with glue

Blush cheeks with marker

Sew on legs

Sew on tail

🌷 *Directions for Fox, Crow, and Backpack on pg. 76*

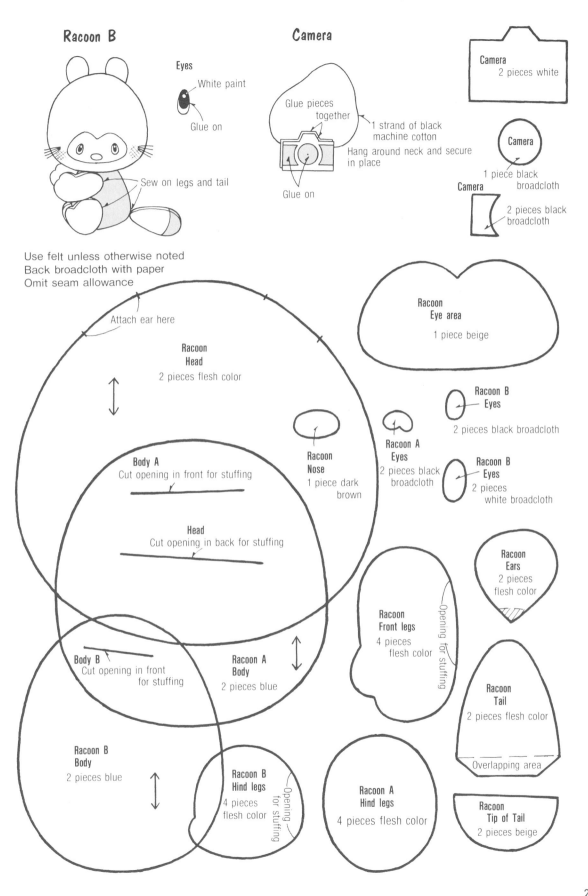

Racoon B

Eyes

White paint

Glue on

Sew on legs and tail

Camera

Glue pieces together

1 strand of black machine cotton

Hang around neck and secure in place

Glue on

Camera
2 pieces white

Camera
1 piece black broadcloth

Camera
2 pieces black broadcloth

Use felt unless otherwise noted
Back broadcloth with paper
Omit seam allowance

Attach ear here

Racoon
Head
2 pieces flesh color

Racoon
Eye area
1 piece beige

Racoon B
Eyes
2 pieces black broadcloth

Body A
Cut opening in front for stuffing

Racoon
Nose
1 piece dark brown

Racoon A
Eyes
2 pieces black broadcloth

Racoon B
Eyes
2 pieces white broadcloth

Head
Cut opening in back for stuffing

Racoon
Ears
2 pieces flesh color

Racoon
Front legs
4 pieces flesh color

Opening for stuffing

Body B
Cut opening in front for stuffing

Racoon A
Body
2 pieces blue

Racoon
Tail
2 pieces flesh color

Racoon B
Body
2 pieces blue

Racoon B
Hind legs
4 pieces flesh color

Opening for stuffing

Racoon A
Hind legs
4 pieces flesh color

Overlapping area

Racoon
Tip of Tail
2 pieces beige

I am
a Ninja

I AM A NINJA

Shown on pgs. 28-29

	Felt	Broadcloth	Machine Cotton	Others (Common Materials)
A	25×20cm(10"×8") deep pink. 15cm(6") square white. 4×11cm(1½"×4½") black. 4×6cm(1½"×2½") each cream, gold.	Scraps of gray, salmon pink.	Deep pink. White	Medium-fine ivory yarn. 20cm(8") black twisted string. Fiberfill. Cement glue. White paint (for B only).
B	25×20cm(10"×8") orange. 15cm(6") square white. 4×11cm(1½"×4½") black. 4×6cm(1½"×2½") each light green, gold.	Scraps of gray, salmon pink.	Orange. White	
C	25×20cm(10"×8") lavender. 4×11cm (1½"×4½") black. 15cm(6") square white. 4×6cm(1½"×2½") each blue, gold.	Scraps of gray, salmon pink.	Lavender. Gray. White	

① Head

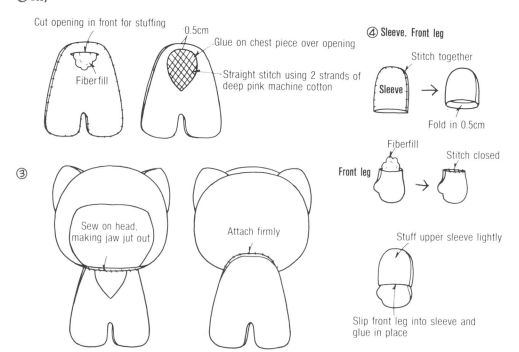

Stitch together

Ear

Stuff lightly

Fold in ears

Hood, front

Face

Glue together

Hood, back

Fiberfill

Stitch front and back hoods together

Cut opening for stuffing

② Body

Cut opening in front for stuffing

Fiberfill

0.5cm

Glue on chest piece over opening

Straight stitch using 2 strands of deep pink machine cotton

④ Sleeve, Front leg

Stitch together

Sleeve

Fold in 0.5cm

③

Sew on head, making jaw jut out

Attach firmly

Fiberfill

Stitch closed

Front leg

Stuff upper sleeve lightly

Slip front leg into sleeve and glue in place

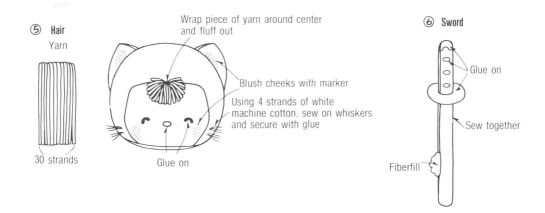

⑤ Hair
Yarn

30 strands

Wrap piece of yarn around center and fluff out

Blush cheeks with marker

Using 4 strands of white machine cotton, sew on whiskers and secure with glue

Glue on

⑥ Sword

Glue on

Sew together

Fiberfill

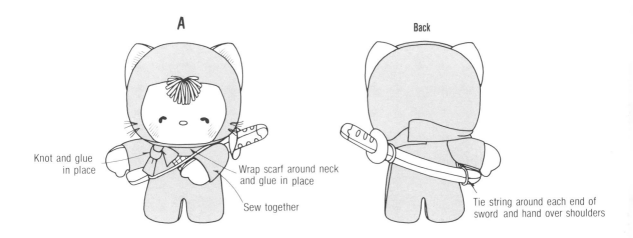

A

Back

Knot and glue in place

Wrap scarf around neck and glue in place

Sew together

Tie string around each end of sword and hand over shoulders

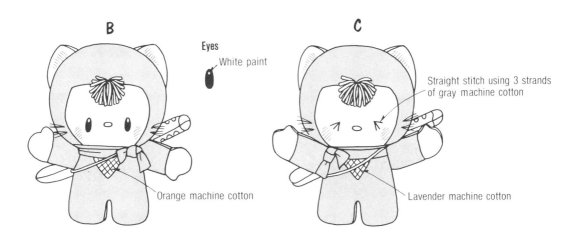

B

Eyes

White paint

Orange machine cotton

C

Straight stitch using 3 strands of gray machine cotton

Lavender machine cotton

🍄 *Patterns on pg. 78*

Friendly Animals

FRIENDLY ANIMALS

Shown on pgs. 32-33

	Felt	Broadcloth	Others	Common Materials
Rabbit	10×15cm(4"×6") white.	Scraps of black, salmon pink.	White machine cotton.	Orange marker. Fiberfill. Cement glue. White paint.
Dog	10×15cm(4"×6") flesh. Scraps of brown.	Scraps of black.	Reddish-brown felt pen.	
Mouse	10cm(4") square cream.	Scraps of black.	Deep pink, White machine cotton.	
Mole	10×6cm(4"×2½") deep pink.	Scraps of black.	Black machine cotton.	
Alligator	10×5cm(4"×2") blue.	Scraps of white, black.	Black machine cotton.	
Panda Bear	12cm(4¾") square white. 7cm(2¾") square gray.	Scraps of black, salmon pink.		
Leopard	10×15cm(4"×6") pale orange. Scraps of deep pink.	Scraps of black.	Flesh machine cotton, Reddish-brown felt pen.	
Cat	13cm(5¼") square pink. 5cm(2") square deep pink.	Scraps of black.	White machine cotton.	
Wolf	13cm(5¼") square brown. Scraps of orange.	Scraps of black.	Black machine cotton.	
Zebra	13cm(5¼") square white. Scraps of gray, pale orange.	Scraps of black, gray.		
Tiger	13cm(5¼") suqare corn yellow. Scraps of orange.	Scraps of black.	Brown felt pen.	
Lion	12cm(4¾") square white. 8cm(3¼") square gray. Scraps of pale orange.	Scraps of black.		
Cow	15cm(6") square white. Scraps of flesh, gray.	Scraps of black.	Gray feltpen.	
Hippo-potamus	20cm(8") square light green. 8cm(3¼") square cream.	Scraps of black.		
Koala Bear	20cm(8") square light brown. Scraps of dark brown.	Scraps of black.	Black machine cotton.	

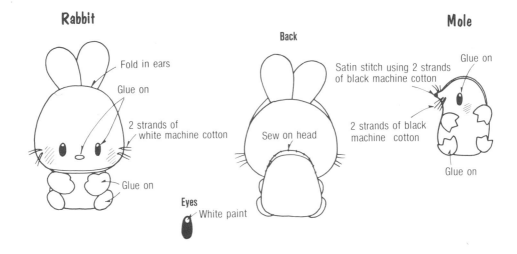

Rabbit

Fold in ears

Glue on

2 strands of white machine cotton

Glue on

Back

Sew on head

Eyes

White paint

Mole

Glue on

Satin stitch using 2 strands of black machine cotton

2 strands of black machine cotton

Glue on

Dog

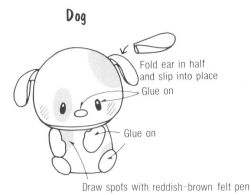

Fold ear in half and slip into place

Glue on

Glue on

Draw spots with reddish-brown felt pen

Mouse

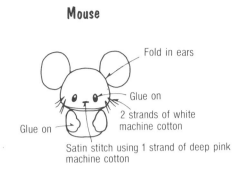

Fold in ears

Glue on

2 strands of white machine cotton

Glue on

Satin stitch using 1 strand of deep pink machine cotton

Alligator

Straight stitch using 2 strands of black machine cotton

Glue on

Panda Bear

Fold in ears and tail

Glue on

Back

Sew on head

Back

Leopard

Draw spots with reddish-brown felt pen

Glue on

2 strands of flesh machine cotton

Glue on

Fold in tail

Cat

Glue on

Slip into place

2 strands of white machine cotton

Wolf

Fold in ears and tail

Glue on

Satin stitch using 2 strands of black machine cotton

Slip into place

🍄 *Directions for Zebra, Tiger, Lion, Cow, Hippopotamus, and Koala Bear on pg. 79*

★ *Patterns for Friendly Animals on pg. 93*

Welcome to
Fantasy Land

WELCOME TO FANTASY LAND *Shown on pgs. 36-37*

☆ ☆ ☆

	Felt	Broadcloth	Medium-fine Yarn	Others	Common Materials
A (A')	$8 \times 12cm(3\frac{1}{4}" \times 4\frac{3}{4}")$ peach. $9 \times 5cm(3\frac{1}{2}" \times 2")$ blue(deep pink). $1 \times 10cm(\frac{3}{8}" \times 4")$ light blue(pink).	Scraps of black	Grayish purple		Fiberfill. Cement glue. White paint. Orange marker.
B	$8 \times 12cm(3\frac{1}{4}" \times 4\frac{3}{4}")$ flesh. $10cm(4")$ square purple, black. $1 \times 10cm(\frac{3}{8}" \times 4")$ deep purple. Scraps of navy, blue, orange.	Scraps of black, white		Orange machine cotton	
C	$8 \times 12cm(3\frac{1}{4}" \times 4\frac{3}{4}")$ peach. $10 \times 5cm(4" \times 2")$ orange. $1 \times 11cm(\frac{3}{8}" \times 4\frac{1}{2}")$ brick red. $1 \times 20cm(\frac{3}{8}" \times 8")$ black. Scraps of light green.	Scraps of black	Brick red	Black machine cotton	
D (E)	$8 \times 12cm(3\frac{1}{4}" \times 4\frac{3}{4}")$ flesh. $10 \times 5cm(4" \times 2")$ gray(brown). $8 \times 3cm(3\frac{1}{4}" \times 1\frac{1}{4}")$ black. $1 \times 10cm(\frac{3}{8}" \times 4")$ dark gray(dark brown).	Scraps of black	Ivory	Brown, beige machine cotton	
F	$8 \times 12cm(3\frac{1}{4}" \times 4\frac{3}{4}")$ flesh. $10cm(4")$ square dark brown. $10 \times 5cm(4" \times 2")$ mustard. $4cm(1\frac{1}{2}")$ square beige.	Scraps of black	Old rose	Dark brown, orange machine cotton	
G	$8 \times 12cm(3\frac{1}{4}" \times 4\frac{3}{4}")$ flesh. $8 \times 5cm(3\frac{1}{4}" \times 2")$ each blue, light green. Scraps of white.	Scraps of black	Ivory		
H	$8 \times 12cm(3\frac{1}{4}" \times 4\frac{3}{4}")$ peach. $6 \times 5cm(2\frac{1}{2}" \times 2")$ each lavender, deep pink. $6 \times 7cm(2\frac{1}{2}" \times 2\frac{3}{4}")$ dark brown. Scraps of white, orange.	Scraps of black, orange	Ivory	Black machine cotton	
I	$13cm(5\frac{1}{4}")$ square flesh. $5 \times 4cm(2" \times 1\frac{1}{2}")$ mustard. $4 \times 3cm(1\frac{1}{2}" \times 1\frac{1}{4}")$ orange.	Scraps of black	Cream	Orange machine cotton Brown felt pen	
J	$13cm(5\frac{1}{4}")$ square flesh. Scraps of pink.	Scraps of black	Cream		
K	$13cm(5\frac{1}{4}")$ square flesh	Scraps of black	Cream		
L	$8 \times 12cm(3\frac{1}{4}" \times 4\frac{3}{4}")$ peach. $8 \times 10cm(3\frac{1}{4}" \times 4")$ gray. Scraps of blue.	Scraps of black, white	Ivory	Lavender embroidery thread. #22 white paper-wrapped wire	
M	$12cm(4\frac{3}{4}")$ square flesh. $5cm(2")$ square pink. Scraps of deep pink, white.	Scraps of black	Ivory		

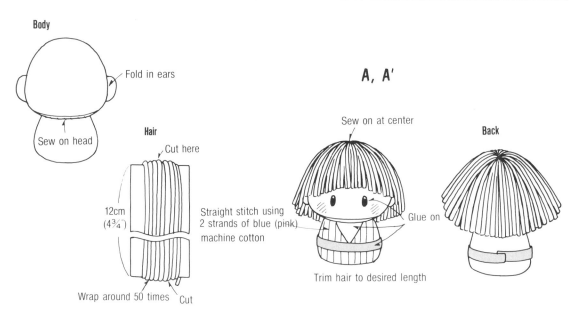

Body

Fold in ears

Sew on head

Hair

Cut here

12cm ($4\frac{3}{4}"$)

Wrap around 50 times   Cut

A, A'

Sew on at center

Straight stitch using 2 strands of blue (pink) machine cotton

Glue on

Trim hair to desired length

Back

B

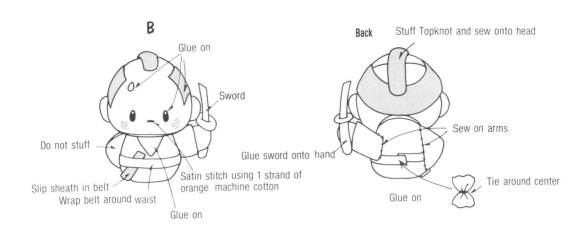

Glue on

Sword

Do not stuff

Slip sheath in belt
Wrap belt around waist

Satin stitch using 1 strand of
orange machine cotton

Glue on

Back   Stuff Topknot and sew onto head

Sew on arms

Glue sword onto hand

Tie around center

Glue on

C

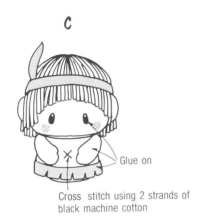

Glue on

Cross stitch using 2 strands of
black machine cotton

D

Straight stitch using 1 strand of
brown machine cotton

Sew on hair

Glue on

Blush cheeks

Glue on vest

Wrap belt around waist   Satin stitch using 2 strands of beige
machine cotton

E

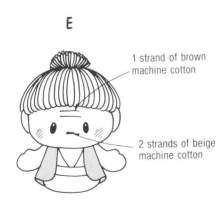

1 strand of brown
machine cotton

2 strands of beige
machine cotton

Back

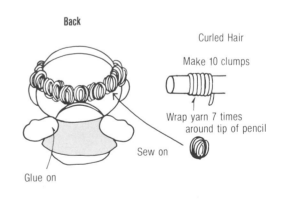

Curled Hair

Make 10 clumps

Wrap yarn 7 times
around tip of pencil

Sew on

Glue on

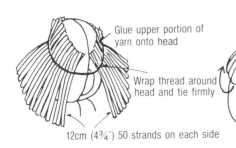

Glue upper portion of
yarn onto head

Trim to form chignon

Turn up hair
and tie off

Wrap thread around
head and tie firmly

12cm (4¾") 50 strands on each side

🍷 *Directions for F–M on pg. 73*

★ *Patterns for Welcome to
Fantasy Land on pg. 98*

Quartet

QUARTET

Shown on pgs. 40-41

	Felt	Ribbon	Others	Common Materials
Boy (Other Boys)	20cm(8") square each flesh, black, gray, white. 11cm(4½") square dark brown.	6cm(2½") of gray, 1.5cm(⅝") in width. (dark green) (dark brown)	2 black buttons, 0.7cm (¼") in diameter (#22 white paper-wrapped wire and black felt pen for glasses).	Reddish-brown medium-fine yarn. Scraps of gray broadcloth. 1 piece of #20 wire. Orange marker. Fiberfill. Cement glue.
Girl	10×30cm(4"×12") flesh. 27cm(10¾") square black. 10×20cm(4"×8") white, dark brown.	8cm(3¼") of red, 2.5cm(1") in width. 50cm(20") of black, 1.5cm(⅝") in width.	10×30cm(4"×12") white broadcloth. 40cm(16") of white lace, 1.5cm(⅝") in width. 40cm(16") of thin rubber tape.	
Instruments	Styrofoam. 4 screw nails of approx. 1cm(⅜") for each instrument. #30 machine cotton, dark brown. #30 white paper-wrapped wire. #20 wire. brown, black watercolor paint. Cement glue. Varnish			

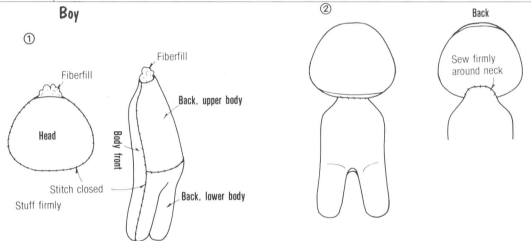

Boy

① Fiberfill / Fiberfill / Back, upper body / Head / Body front / Back, lower body / Stitch closed / Stuff firmly

② Back / Sew firmly around neck

③ Pants — Pants, front / Pants, back, hip / Pants, back, legs / Stitch together

④ Jacket — Sew on lapels and smooth with iron / Label / Jacket front / Jacket, back (wrong side) / Jacket front (right side) / Stitch sides closed

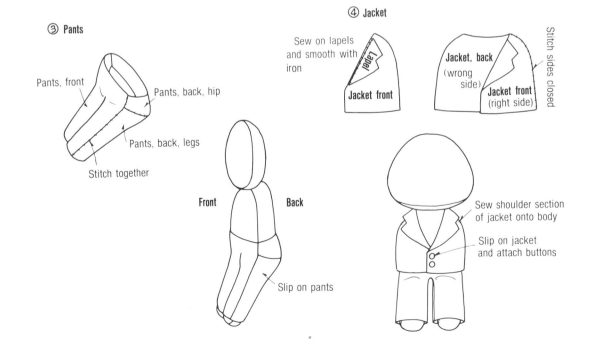

Front / Back / Slip on pants

Sew shoulder section of jacket onto body / Slip on jacket and attach buttons

⑤ Hand, Sleeve

Fiberfill

Sleeve

Stitch closed

Stuff

Hand

→

Slip hand into sleeve and secure in place with glue

Attach sleeves, sewing through to body

⑥ Hair

Lower section

Top section

14cm (5½")

9.5cm (3¾")

Wrap around 90 times

Wrap around 50 times

Sew on lower and top sections of hair by backstitching at center

Cut one end

Fluff out hair and cut into layers Smooth cement glue evenly over hair

⑦ Shoes

Stuff and close

Stitch together

Cut opening in top side of shoe

Sew on leg over opening

⑧ Bow Tie

1.5cm (⅝")

10cm (4") in length

Tie thread around center

Glasses

Shape round frames by wrapping wire around pencil

5cm (2")

1.3cm (½")

Color #22 paper-wrapped wire with black felt pen

Right Arm, back

Intertwine 2 #20 wires and attach onto arm with thread ; bend arm as shown

Glue on

Blush cheeks

Sew on tie (gray, dark green)

Sew bow onto hand

Insert wire ends of glasses into face and secure with glue

(Dark brown)

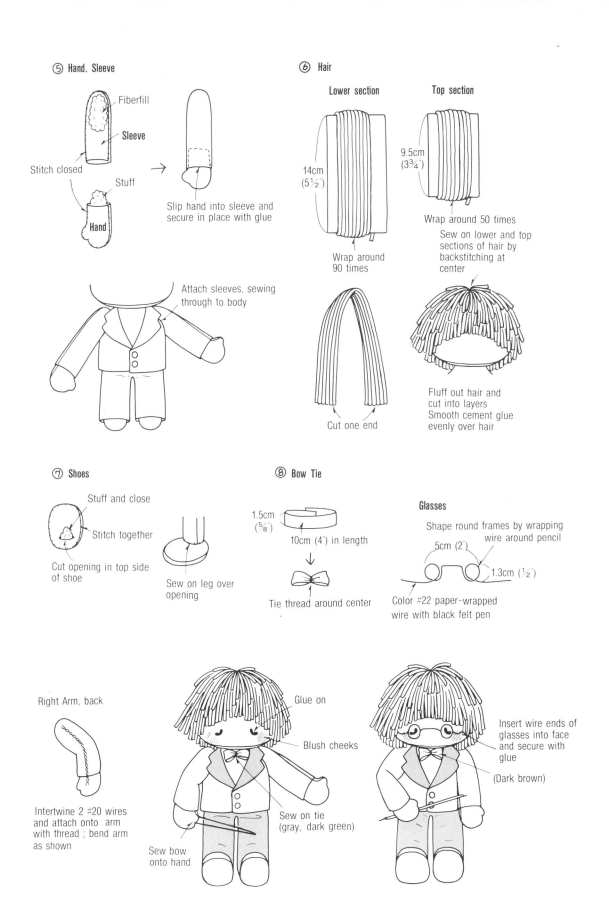

🍄 *Directions for Girl and Instruments, patterns all on pg. 80*

Football

FOOTBALL

Shown on pgs. 44-45

☆ ☆ ☆

	Felt	Broadcloth	Medium-Fine Yarn	Others (Common Materials)
A	20×15cm(8"×6") cherry pink. 20×12cm (8"×4¾") flesh. 10×15cm(4"×6") white. 10cm(4") square beige. Scraps of orange.	Scraps of white, orange	Ivory	Fiberfill. Orange marker Pale orange machine cotton. Cement glue.
B	20×13cm(8"×5¼") bright yellow. 20×12cm (8"×4¾") flesh. 20×10cm(8"×4") orange. 10cm(4") square beige.	Scraps of white	Ivory	
C	20cm(8") square blue. 20×12cm(8"×4¾") flesh. 10cm(4") square each light green, beige. Scraps of orange.	Scraps of white	Ivory	
D	20×15cm(8"×6") pink, lavender. 20×12cm(8"×4¾") flesh. 10cm(4") square beige. Scraps of orange.	Scraps of white	Ivory	
Football	7×10cm(2¾"×4") brown. 5cm(2") square dark brown.			Fiberfill. Cement glue.

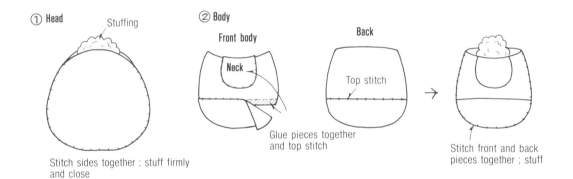

① Head

Stuffing

Stitch sides together ; stuff firmly and close

② Body

Front body

Neck

Glue pieces together and top stitch

Back

Top stitch

→

Stitch front and back pieces together ; stuff

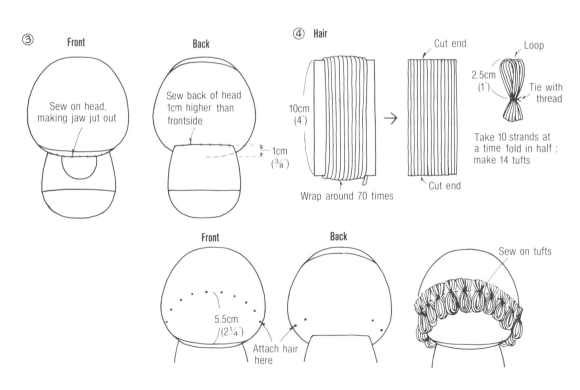

③ Front

Sew on head, making jaw jut out

Back

Sew back of head 1cm higher than frontside

1cm (⅜")

④ Hair

10cm (4")

Wrap around 70 times

Cut end

Cut end

Loop

2.5cm (1")

Tie with thread

Take 10 strands at a time fold in half ; make 14 tufts

Front

5.5cm (2¼")

Attach hair here

Back

Sew on tufts

⑤ **Helmet**

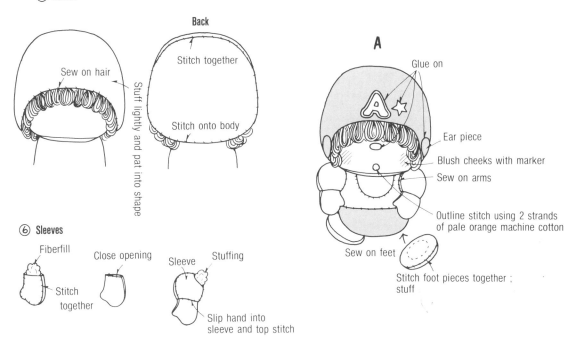

Back

Sew on hair

Stitch together

Stitch onto body

Stuff lightly and pat into shape

A

Glue on

Ear piece

Blush cheeks with marker

Sew on arms

Outline stitch using 2 strands of pale orange machine cotton

Sew on feet

Stitch foot pieces together ; stuff

⑥ **Sleeves**

Fiberfill

Stitch together

Close opening

Sleeve   Stuffing

Slip hand into sleeve and top stitch

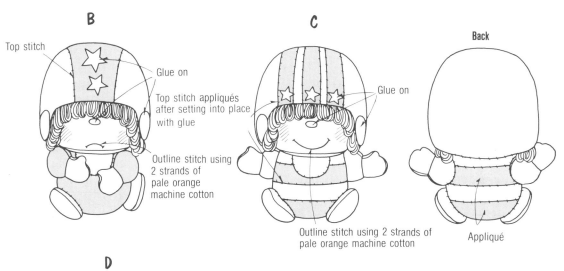

B

Top stitch

Glue on

Top stitch appliqués after setting into place with glue

Outline stitch using 2 strands of pale orange machine cotton

C

Glue on

Outline stitch using 2 strands of pale orange machine cotton

Back

Appliqué

D

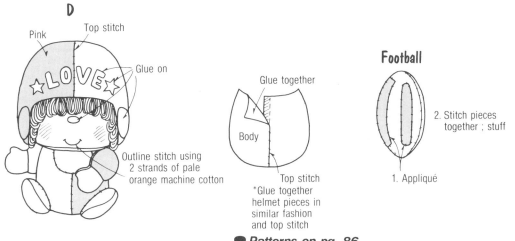

Pink   Top stitch

Glue on

☆LOVE☆

Outline stitch using 2 strands of pale orange machine cotton

Glue together

Body

Top stitch
*Glue together helmet pieces in similar fashion and top stitch

Football

2. Stitch pieces together ; stuff

1. Appliqué

🍄 *Patterns on pg. 86*

BIRTHDAY PARTY

Shown on pgs. 48-49

☆ ☆ ☆

	Felt	Medium–Fine Yarn	Others
A	13×10cm(5¼"×4") deep pink. 17×10cm(6¾"×4") flesh. 5×3cm(2"×1¼") brown.	Tomato red	Scraps of black broadcloth. Fiberfill. Cement glue. White paint. Orange marker.
B	13×10cm(5¼"×4") pale green. Flesh, brown same as for A.	Olive green	Fiberfill. Cement glue. Black machine cotton. Orange marker.
C	13×10cm(5¼"×4") pale orange. 20×1cm(8"×⅜") blue. Flesh, brown same as for A.	Bright yellow	Same as for A.
D	13×10cm(5¼"×4") gray. Flesh, brown same as for A.	Gray	Same as for A.
E	13×10cm(5¼"×4") purple. Flesh, brown same as for A.	Reddish purple	Same as for A. Black machine cotton.
F	13×10cm(5¼"×4") soft pink. 5×3cm(2"×1¼") tomato red. Flesh, brown same as for A.	Pink	Same as for A. Black machine cotton.

Use felt unless otherwise noted

Back broadcloth with paper

Omit seam allowance

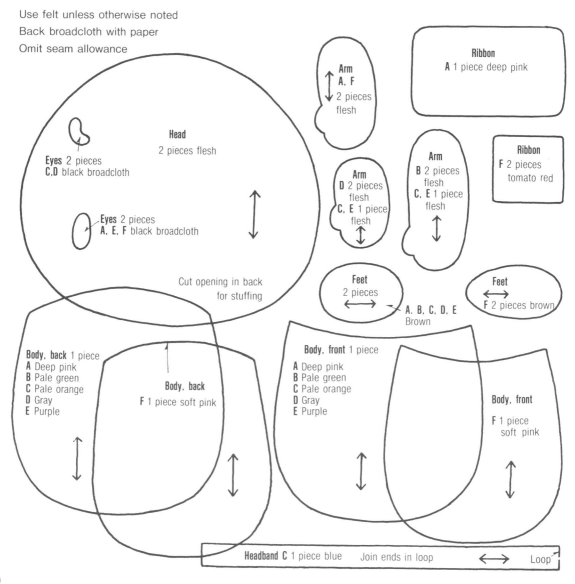

Arm
A, F
2 pieces
flesh

Ribbon
A 1 piece deep pink

Eyes 2 pieces
C,D black broadcloth

Head
2 pieces flesh

Arm
D 2 pieces
flesh
C, E 1 piece
flesh

Arm
B 2 pieces
flesh
C, E 1 piece
flesh

Ribbon
F 2 pieces
tomato red

Eyes 2 pieces
A, E, F black broadcloth

Cut opening in back
for stuffing

Feet
2 pieces

Feet
F 2 pieces brown

A, B, C, D, E
Brown

Body, back 1 piece
A Deep pink
B Pale green
C Pale orange
D Gray
E Purple

Body, back
F 1 piece soft pink

Body, front 1 piece
A Deep pink
B Pale green
C Pale orange
D Gray
E Purple

Body, front
F 1 piece
soft pink

Headband C 1 piece blue   Join ends in loop   Loop

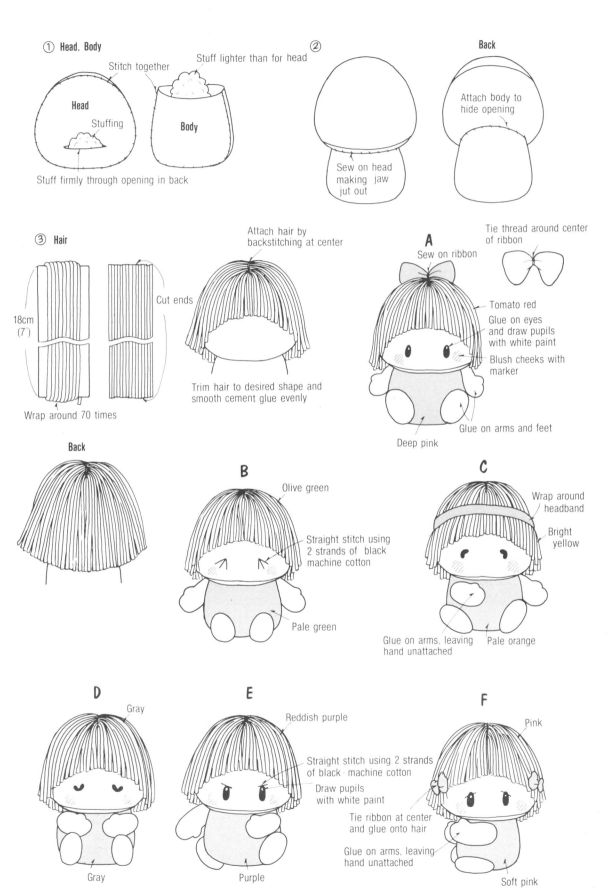

① Head, Body

Stitch together

Stuff lighter than for head

Head

Stuffing

Body

Stuff firmly through opening in back

②

Back

Attach body to hide opening

Sew on head making jaw jut out

③ Hair

Attach hair by backstitching at center

18cm (7")

Cut ends

Wrap around 70 times

Trim hair to desired shape and smooth cement glue evenly

A

Sew on ribbon

Tie thread around center of ribbon

Tomato red

Glue on eyes and draw pupils with white paint

Blush cheeks with marker

Glue on arms and feet

Deep pink

Back

B

Olive green

Straight stitch using 2 strands of black machine cotton

Pale green

C

Wrap around headband

Bright yellow

Glue on arms, leaving hand unattached

Pale orange

D

Gray

Gray

E

Reddish purple

Straight stitch using 2 strands of black machine cotton

Draw pupils with white paint

Tie ribbon at center and glue onto hair

Glue on arms, leaving hand unattached

Purple

F

Pink

Soft pink

51

LONESOME COWBOY

LONESOME COWBOY

Shown on pgs. 52-53

☆   ☆   ☆

	Felt	Broadcloth	Others
Cowboy	20cm(8") square fresh. 13×20cm (5¼"×8") blue. 20×25cm(8"×10") brown. 4×10cm(1½"×4") pale blue.	Scraps of white, gray	20×17cm(8"×6¾") checked biera fabric. 30cm(12") of reddish brown ribbon. 0.8cm(⅜") in width. Pale brown loop yarn. gray machine cotton. White paint. Brown, Orange markers. Fiberfill. Cement glue.
Frog, large (small)	23×17cm(9"×6¾") light green. [17×15cm(6¾"×6")] 8×10cm(3¼"×4") white [6×8cm(2½"×3¼")]	Scraps of white, gray	Orange embroidery thread. Fiberfill. Cement glue.
Horse	20×30cm(8"×12") beige. 10cm(4") square each brown,white.	Scraps of gray	40cm(16") of cotton string. Fiberfill. Cement glue.

① **Head, Body**

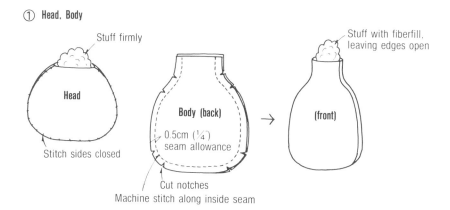

②

③ **Hair**   **Loop yarn**

④ **Legs**

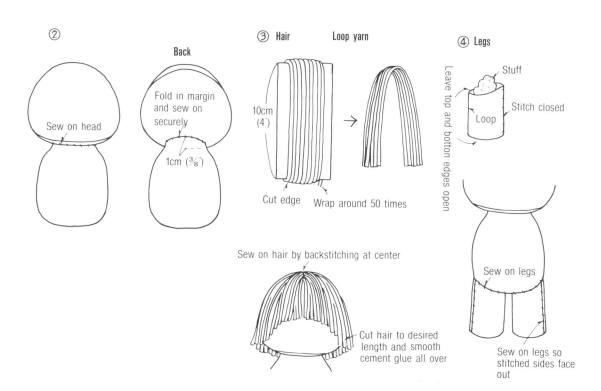

54

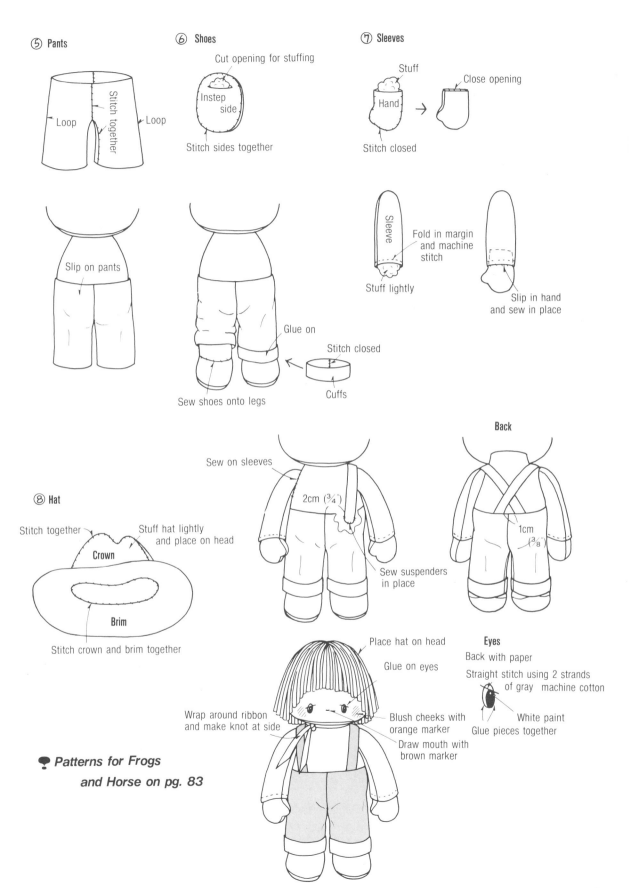

⑤ Pants

Loop — Stitch together — Loop

Slip on pants

Sew shoes onto legs

Glue on
Stitch closed
Cuffs

⑥ Shoes

Cut opening for stuffing

Instep side

Stitch sides together

⑦ Sleeves

Stuff

Hand

Stitch closed

Close opening

Sleeve

Fold in margin and machine stitch

Stuff lightly

Slip in hand and sew in place

⑧ Hat

Stitch together

Stuff hat lightly and place on head

Crown

Brim

Stitch crown and brim together

Sew on sleeves

2cm (³⁄₄")

Sew suspenders in place

Back

1cm (³⁄₈")

Place hat on head

Glue on eyes

Wrap around ribbon and make knot at side

Blush cheeks with orange marker

Draw mouth with brown marker

Eyes

Back with paper

Straight stitch using 2 strands of gray machine cotton

White paint

Glue pieces together

🍄 **Patterns for Frogs and Horse on pg. 83**

55

Summer Vacation

SUMMER VACATION

Shown on pgs. 56-57

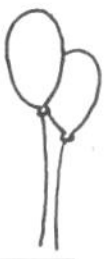

☆ ☆ ☆

	Cotton Jerseys	Broadcloth	Yarn	Others
A	22×27cm(8¾" ×10¾")flesh	20cm(8") square white-on-pink polka dots. 18cm(7") square white. Scraps of gray, salmon pink.	Medium-fine bright yellow	White paint
B	22×25cm(8¾" ×10")flesh	25×10cm(10"×4") red and white stripes. 10×20cm(4"×8") white. 16×17cm(6¼"×6¾") red. Scraps of gray, black, salmon pink.	Medium-fine reddish brown	Scraps of orange felt
C	22×27cm(8¾" ×10¾")flesh	20×7cm(8"×2¾") pink and white stripes. 20cm(8") square white. Scraps of gray, salmon pink.	Medium-fine ivory	Scraps of white felt. White embroidery thread.1 white round bead.15cm(6") of elastic tape. 20cm(8") of pink ribbon 0.3cm(⅛") in width.
D	22×25cm(8¾" ×10")flesh	20×17cm(8"×6¾") blue. 10×20cm (4"×8") white. 20×7cm(8"×2¾") blue and white stripes. Scraps of gray, salmon pink.	Medium-fine reddish purple	1 # 20white paper-wrapped wire.
Common Materials	Fiberfill. Orange, brown markers. Cement glue.			

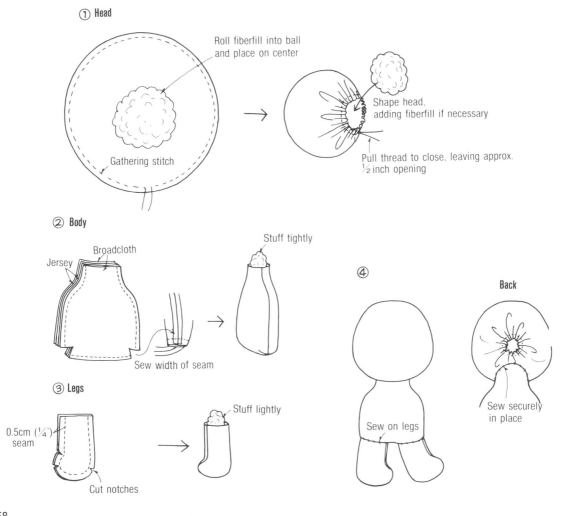

① **Head**

Roll fiberfill into ball and place on center

Gathering stitch

Shape head, adding fiberfill if necessary

Pull thread to close, leaving approx. ½ inch opening

② **Body**

Jersey

Broadcloth

Stuff tightly

Sew width of seam

③ **Legs**

0.5cm (¼") seam

Cut notches

Stuff lightly

④

Back

Sew on legs

Sew securely in place

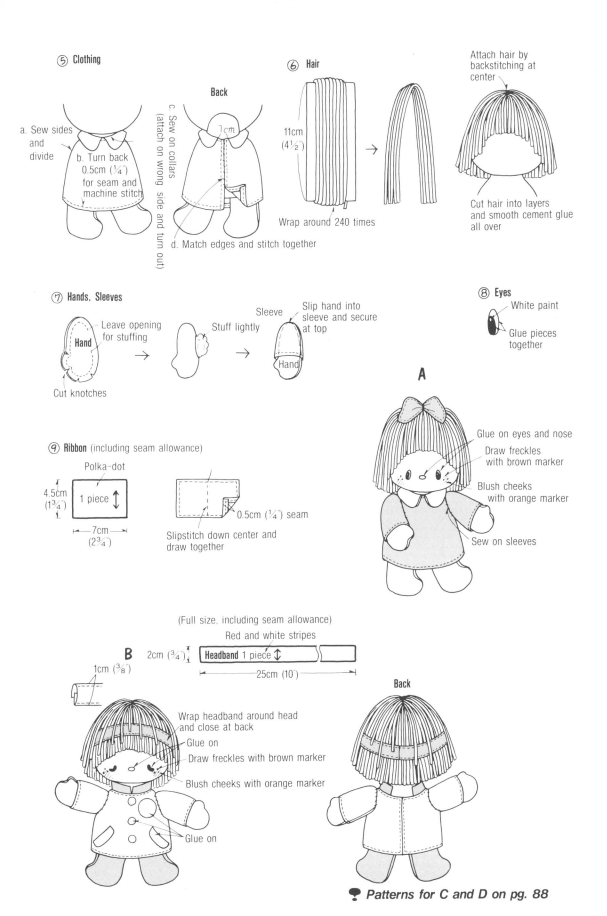

⑤ Clothing

a. Sew sides and divide

b. Turn back 0.5cm (¼") for seam and machine stitch

Back

1cm

c. Sew on collars (attach on wrong side and turn out)

d. Match edges and stitch together

⑥ Hair

11cm (4½")

Wrap around 240 times

Attach hair by backstitching at center

Cut hair into layers and smooth cement glue all over

⑦ Hands, Sleeves

Hand

Leave opening for stuffing

Cut knotches

Stuff lightly

Sleeve

Slip hand into sleeve and secure at top

Hand

⑧ Eyes

White paint

Glue pieces together

⑨ Ribbon (including seam allowance)

Polka-dot

4.5cm (1¾")

1 piece ↕

←7cm→ (2¾")

0.5cm (¼") seam

Slipstitch down center and draw together

A

Glue on eyes and nose

Draw freckles with brown marker

Blush cheeks with orange marker

Sew on sleeves

B

(Full size, including seam allowance)
Red and white stripes

2cm (¾")

Headband 1 piece ↕

25cm (10")

1cm (⅜")

Wrap headband around head and close at back

Glue on

Draw freckles with brown marker

Blush cheeks with orange marker

Glue on

Back

🍄 *Patterns for C and D on pg. 88*

Sweet Dreams

SWEET DREAMS

Shown on pgs. 60-61

☆ ☆ ☆

	Felt	Broadcloth	Medium-fine Yarn	Others
Boy	25×38cm(10"×15") flesh. Scraps of salmon pink.	30×40cm(12"×16")lavender. Scraps of gray.	Ivory White	1m(40") purple bias tape
Bedspread		50cm(20") square white.		75cm(29½") white lace. 2.5cm(1") in width. Fiberfill.
Sleeping Boy	20cm(8") square white. 12×16cm(4¾"×6¼") flesh. 5×9cm(2"×3½") wine red. Scraps of salmon pink.	Scraps of gray.	Ivory	10cm(4") orange ribbon. 0.6cm(¼") in width. 1 sequin.
Bride	20cm(8") square white. 12×16cm(4¾"×6¼") flesh. 5×9cm(2"×3½) deep pink.	Scraps of gray.	Ivory	5 tiny artificial flowers. 50cm(20") white lace. 1.2cm (½") in width. 6×22cm(2½"× 8¾") white tulle.
Common Materials (Bedspread excluded)	Orange marker. Fiberfill. Cement glue			

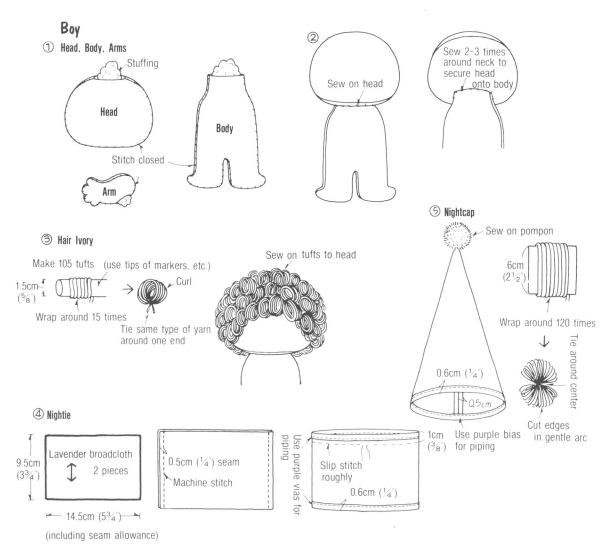

Boy

① Head, Body, Arms

Stuffing

Head

Stitch closed

Arm

Body

② Sew on head

Sew 2-3 times around neck to secure head onto body

③ Hair Ivory

Make 105 tufts (use tips of markers, etc.)

1.5cm (⅝")

Wrap around 15 times

→ Curl

Tie same type of yarn around one end

Sew on tufts to head

⑤ Nightcap

Sew on pompon

6cm (2½")

Wrap around 120 times

↓

Tie around center

Cut edges in gentle arc

0.6cm (¼")

0.5cm

④ Nightie

9.5cm (3¾")

Lavender broadcloth 2 pieces

⇕

14.5cm (5¾")

(including seam allowance)

0.5cm (¼") seam

Machine stitch

Use purple vias for piping

Slip stitch roughly

0.6cm (¼")

1cm (⅜") Use purple bias for piping

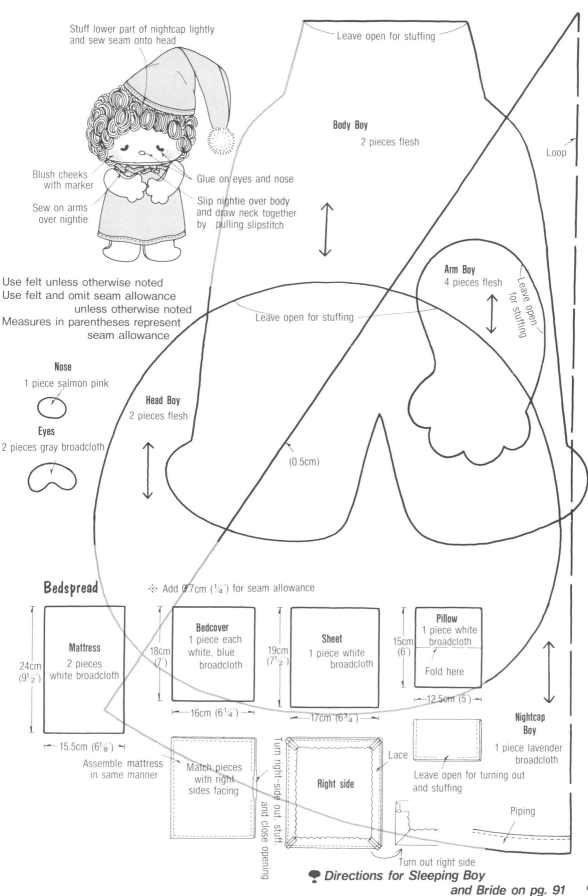

Stuff lower part of nightcap lightly
and sew seam onto head

Leave open for stuffing

Body Boy

2 pieces flesh

Loop

Blush cheeks
with marker

Glue on eyes and nose

Sew on arms
over nightie

Slip nightie over body
and draw neck together
by pulling slipstitch

Arm Boy

4 pieces flesh

Leave open
for stuffing

Use felt unless otherwise noted
Use felt and omit seam allowance
unless otherwise noted
Measures in parentheses represent
seam allowance

Leave open for stuffing

Nose

1 piece salmon pink

Head Boy

2 pieces flesh

(0.5cm)

Eyes

2 pieces gray broadcloth

Bedspread

※ Add 0.7cm (¼") for seam allowance

Mattress

2 pieces
white broadcloth

24cm
(9½")

18cm
(7")

Bedcover

1 piece each
white, blue
broadcloth

19cm
(7½")

Sheet

1 piece white
broadcloth

15cm
(6")

Pillow

1 piece white
broadcloth

Fold here

Nightcap
Boy

1 piece lavender
broadcloth

15.5cm (6⅛")

16cm (6¼")

17cm (6¾")

12.5cm (5")

Assemble mattress
in same manner

Match pieces
with right
sides facing

Turn right side out, stuff, and close opening

Right side

Lace

Leave open for turning out
and stuffing

Piping

Turn out right side

♥ **Directions for Sleeping Boy**
and Bride on pg. 91

and Bride on pg. 91

63

Little Witches

Instructions and Actual-size Patterns

LITTLE WITCHES ☆ ☆ ☆

Shown on pg. 64

	Felt	Cotton Jersey	Satin Fabric	Medium-fine Yarn	Others (Common Materials)
A	10×13cm(4"×5¼") lavender. Scraps of flesh.	12cm(4¾") square flesh	20×30cm (8"×12") black	Rose	Fiberfill. Orange marker. Orange machine cotton. Cement glue.
B	10×13cm(4"×5¼")light green. Scraps of flesh.	12cm(4¾") square flesh	20×30cm (8"×12") black	Beige	
C	10×13cm(4"×5¼") pink. Scraps of flesh.	12cm(4¾") square flesh	20×30cm (8"×12") black	Ivory	
D	10×13cm(4"×5¼") blue. Scraps of flesh.	12cm(4¾") square flesh	20×30cm (8"×12") black	Gray	

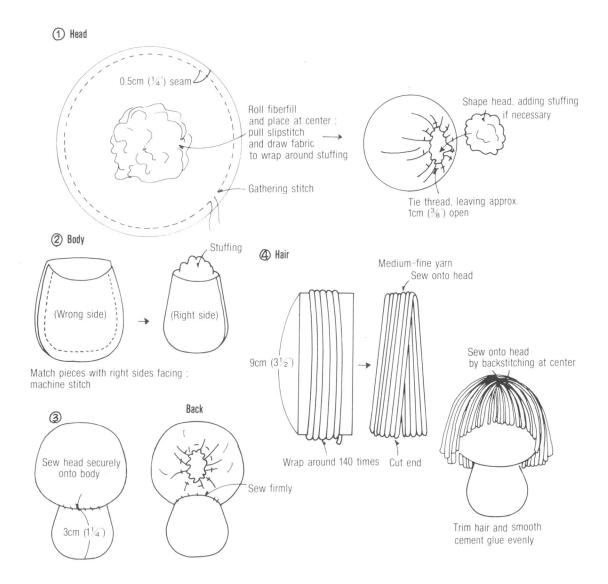

① Head

0.5cm (¼") seam

Roll fiberfill and place at center ; pull slipstitch and draw fabric to wrap around stuffing

Gathering stitch

Shape head, adding stuffing if necessary

Tie thread, leaving approx. 1cm (⅜") open

② Body

Stuffing

(Wrong side) → (Right side)

Match pieces with right sides facing ; machine stitch

③ Sew head securely onto body

3cm (1¼")

Back

Sew firmly

④ Hair

Medium-fine yarn Sew onto head

9cm (3½")

Wrap around 140 times   Cut end

Sew onto head by backstitching at center

Trim hair and smooth cement glue evenly

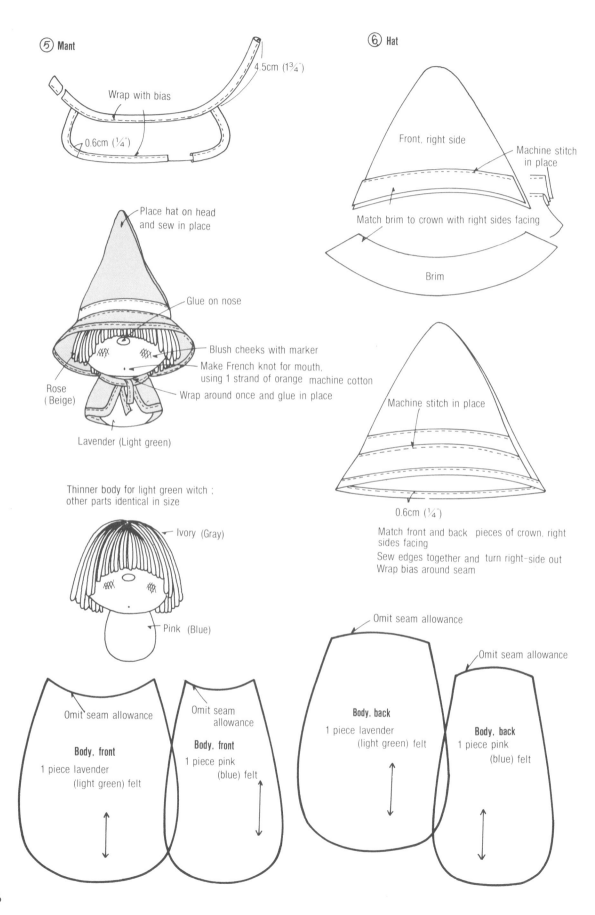

⑤ Mant

4.5cm (1¾")

Wrap with bias

0.6cm (¼")

Place hat on head and sew in place

Glue on nose

Blush cheeks with marker

Make French knot for mouth, using 1 strand of orange machine cotton

Wrap around once and glue in place

Rose (Beige)

Lavender (Light green)

Thinner body for light green witch ; other parts identical in size

Ivory (Gray)

Pink (Blue)

Omit seam allowance

Body, front
1 piece lavender (light green) felt

Omit seam allowance

Body, front
1 piece pink (blue) felt

⑥ Hat

Front, right side

Machine stitch in place

Match brim to crown with right sides facing

Brim

Machine stitch in place

0.6cm (¼")

Match front and back pieces of crown, right sides facing
Sew edges together and turn right-side out
Wrap bias around seam

Omit seam allowance

Omit seam allowance

Body, back
1 piece lavender (light green) felt

Body, back
1 piece pink (blue) felt

Add 0.5cm (¼") for seam allowance except where piping is indicated

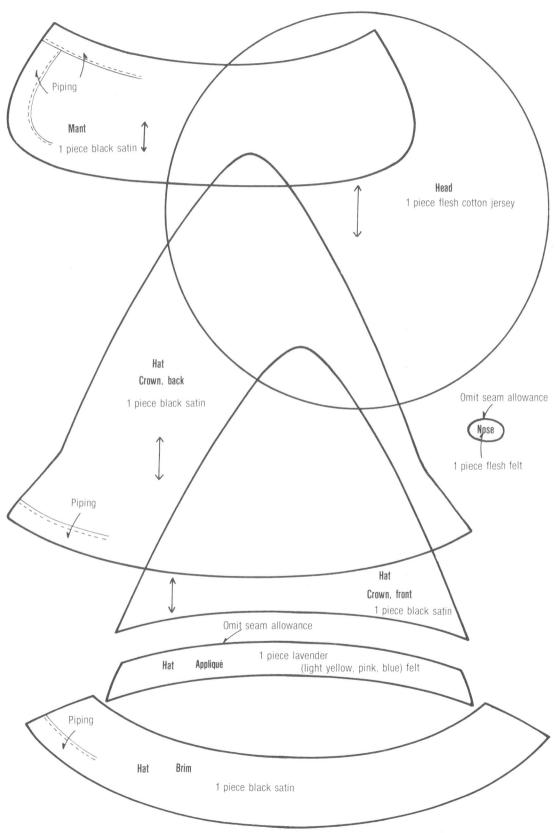

Piping

Mant
1 piece black satin

Head
1 piece flesh cotton jersey

Hat
Crown, back

1 piece black satin

Omit seam allowance

Nose

1 piece flesh felt

Piping

Hat   **Crown, front**

1 piece black satin

Omit seam allowance

Hat   **Appliqué**   1 piece lavender
(light yellow, pink, blue) felt

Piping

Hat   **Brim**

1 piece black satin

Continued from pg.14 *(LITTLE FARMERS)*

Elephant

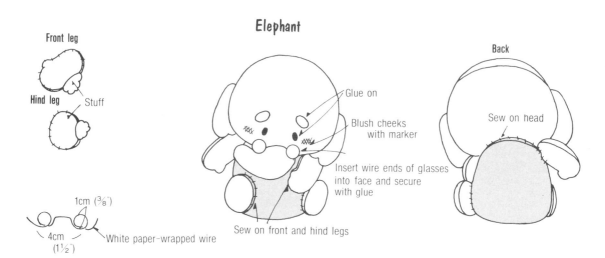

Front leg

Hind leg — Stuff

1cm (³⁄₈″)
4cm (1½″) — White paper-wrapped wire

Glue on

Blush cheeks with marker

Insert wire ends of glasses into face and secure with glue

Sew on front and hind legs

Back

Sew on head

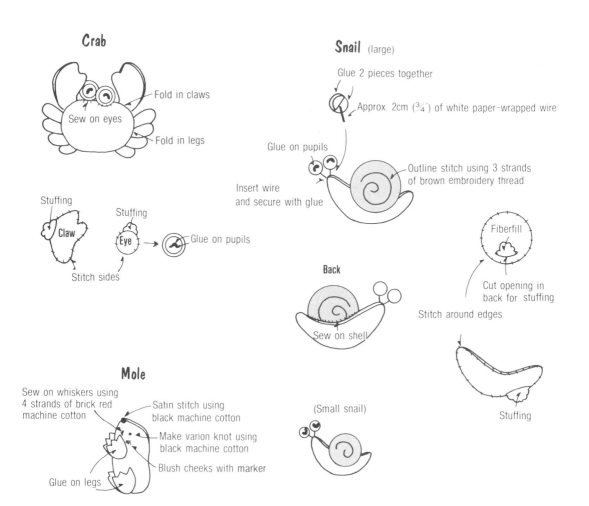

Crab

Fold in claws

Sew on eyes

Fold in legs

Stuffing
Claw
Stitch sides

Stuffing
Eye → Glue on pupils

Snail (large)

Glue 2 pieces together

Approx. 2cm (³⁄₄″) of white paper-wrapped wire

Glue on pupils

Outline stitch using 3 strands of brown embroidery thread

Insert wire and secure with glue

Fiberfill

Cut opening in back for stuffing

Stitch around edges

Back

Sew on shell

Stuffing

Mole

Sew on whiskers using 4 strands of brick red machine cotton

Satin stitch using black machine cotton

Make varion knot using black machine cotton

Blush cheeks with marker

Glue on legs

(Small snail)

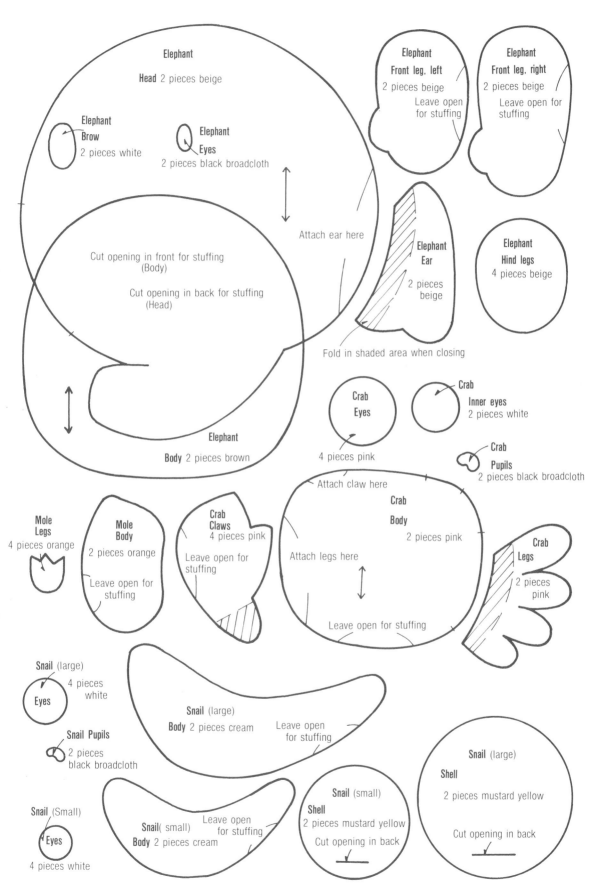

Elephant

Head 2 pieces beige

Elephant
Brow
2 pieces white

Elephant
Eyes
2 pieces black broadcloth

Elephant
Front leg, left
2 pieces beige
Leave open for stuffing

Elephant
Front leg, right
2 pieces beige
Leave open for stuffing

Cut opening in front for stuffing
(Body)

Cut opening in back for stuffing
(Head)

Attach ear here

Elephant
Ear
2 pieces beige

Elephant
Hind legs
4 pieces beige

Fold in shaded area when closing

Elephant
Body 2 pieces brown

Crab
Eyes
4 pieces pink

Crab
Inner eyes
2 pieces white

Crab
Pupils
2 pieces black broadcloth

Attach claw here

Crab
Body
2 pieces pink

Attach legs here

Crab
Legs
2 pieces pink

Mole
Legs
4 pieces orange

Mole
Body
2 pieces orange

Leave open for stuffing

Crab
Claws
4 pieces pink

Leave open for stuffing

Leave open for stuffing

Snail (large)
4 pieces white
Eyes

Snail (large)
Body 2 pieces cream

Leave open for stuffing

Snail Pupils
2 pieces black broadcloth

Snail (large)
Shell
2 pieces mustard yellow

Cut opening in back

Snail (Small)
Eyes
4 pieces white

Snail (small)
Body 2 pieces cream

Leave open for stuffing

Snail (small)
Shell
2 pieces mustard yellow

Cut opening in back

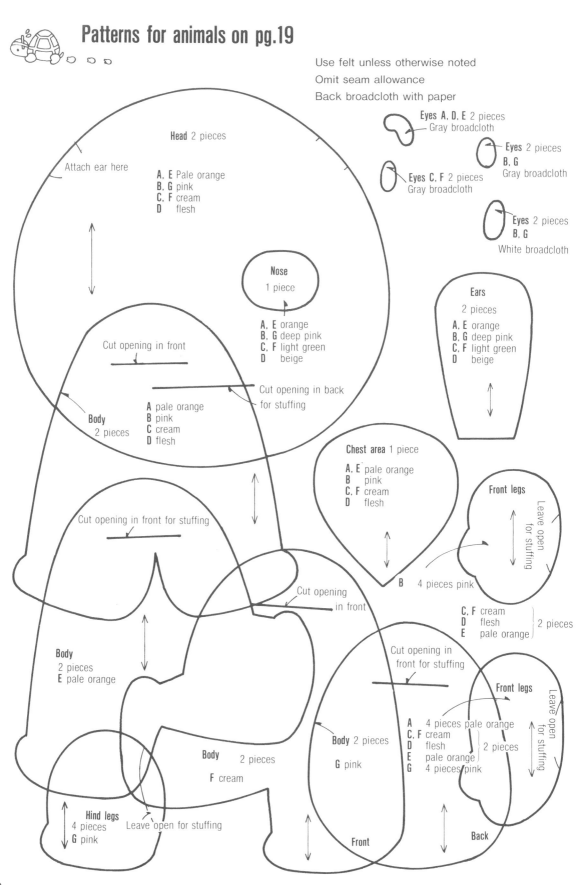

Patterns for animals on pg.19

Use felt unless otherwise noted

Omit seam allowance

Back broadcloth with paper

Head 2 pieces

Attach ear here

A, E Pale orange
B, G pink
C, F cream
D flesh

Eyes A, D, E 2 pieces
Gray broadcloth

Eyes 2 pieces
B, G
Gray broadcloth

Eyes C, F 2 pieces
Gray broadcloth

Eyes 2 pieces
B, G
White broadcloth

Nose
1 piece

A, E orange
B, G deep pink
C, F light green
D beige

Ears
2 pieces

A, E orange
B, G deep pink
C, F light green
D beige

Cut opening in front

Cut opening in back
for stuffing

Body
2 pieces

A pale orange
B pink
C cream
D flesh

Chest area 1 piece

A, E pale orange
B pink
C, F cream
D flesh

Front legs

Leave open
for stuffing

B 4 pieces pink

C, F cream
D flesh } 2 pieces
E pale orange

Cut opening in front for stuffing

Cut opening
in front

Body
2 pieces
E pale orange

Cut opening in
front for stuffing

Front legs

Leave open
for stuffing

Body 2 pieces

G pink

A 4 pieces pale orange
C, F cream
D flesh } 2 pieces
E pale orange
G 4 pieces pink

Body 2 pieces

F cream

Hind legs
4 pieces
G pink

Leave open for stuffing

Front

Back

70

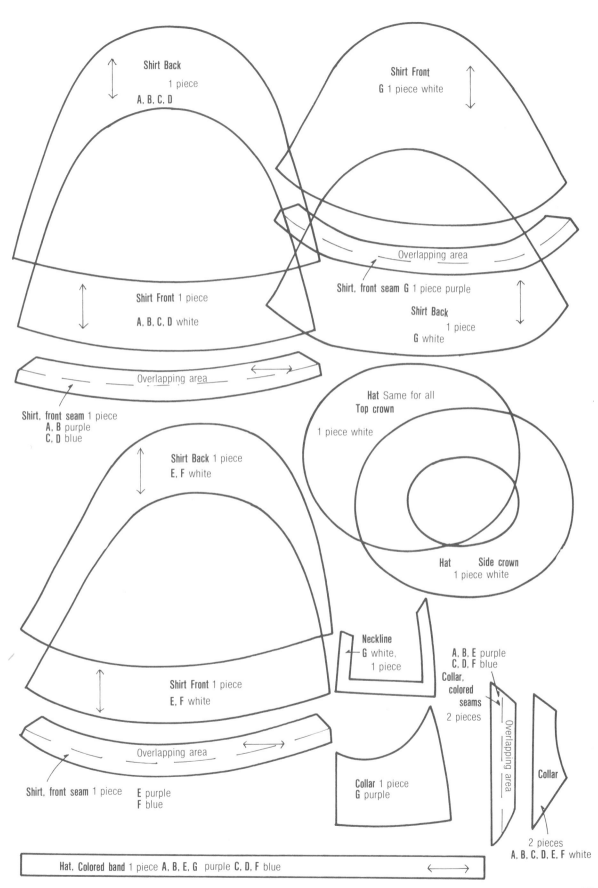

Shirt Back
1 piece
A, B, C, D

Shirt Front
G 1 piece white

Overlapping area

Shirt, front seam G 1 piece purple

Shirt Back
1 piece
G white

Shirt Front 1 piece
A, B, C, D white

Overlapping area

Shirt, front seam 1 piece
A, B purple
C, D blue

Hat Same for all
Top crown

1 piece white

Shirt Back 1 piece
E, F white

Hat   Side crown
1 piece white

Shirt Front 1 piece
E, F white

Neckline
G white,
1 piece

A, B, E purple
C, D, F blue

Collar,
colored
seams
2 pieces

Overlapping area

Collar

Overlapping area

Shirt, front seam 1 piece   E purple
F blue

Collar 1 piece
G purple

2 pieces
A, B, C, D, E, F white

Hat, Colored band 1 piece A, B, E, G purple C, D, F blue

71

Continued from pg.22 *(ICE SPORTS)*

Polar Bear

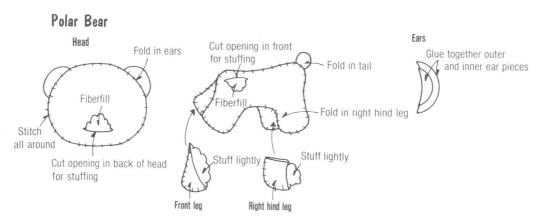

Head

Fold in ears

Fiberfill

Stitch all around

Cut opening in back of head for stuffing

Cut opening in front for stuffing

Fold in tail

Fiberfill

Fold in right hind leg

Stuff lightly

Stuff lightly

Front leg

Right hind leg

Ears

Glue together outer and inner ear pieces

Glue eyes and nose

Wrap around headband

Blush cheeks

Back

Glue on knot

Sew head to Body

Polar Bear

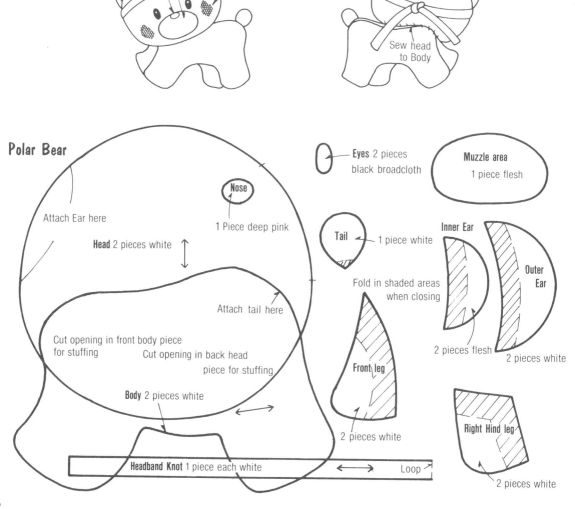

Attach Ear here

Nose

1 Piece deep pink

Head 2 pieces white

Attach tail here

Cut opening in front body piece for stuffing

Cut opening in back head piece for stuffing

Body 2 pieces white

Headband Knot 1 piece each white

Loop

Eyes 2 pieces black broadcloth

Muzzle area 1 piece flesh

Tail 1 piece white

Inner Ear

Fold in shaded areas when closing

2 pieces flesh

Outer Ear

2 pieces white

Front leg

2 pieces white

Right Hind leg

2 pieces white

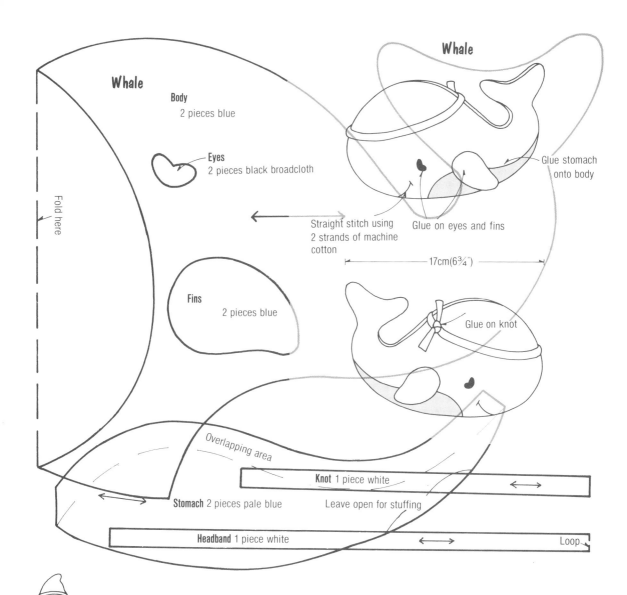

Whale

Whale

Body
2 pieces blue

Eyes
2 pieces black broadcloth

Glue stomach onto body

Straight stitch using 2 strands of machine cotton

Glue on eyes and fins

17cm(6¾")

Fins
2 pieces blue

Glue on knot

Overlapping area

Knot 1 piece white

Leave open for stuffing

Stomach 2 pieces pale blue

Headband 1 piece white

Loop

Continued from pg. 39 *(WELCOME TO FANTASY LAND)*

☆   ☆   ☆

Patterns on pg. 98

F

Place Hat on head

Topstitch brown patch

Satin stitch using 2 strands of orange machine cotton

Glue on

Roll and glue onto hand

G

Fold in upper part of Hat

Fold between tip and glue in place

Glue on

Glue right and left pieces together

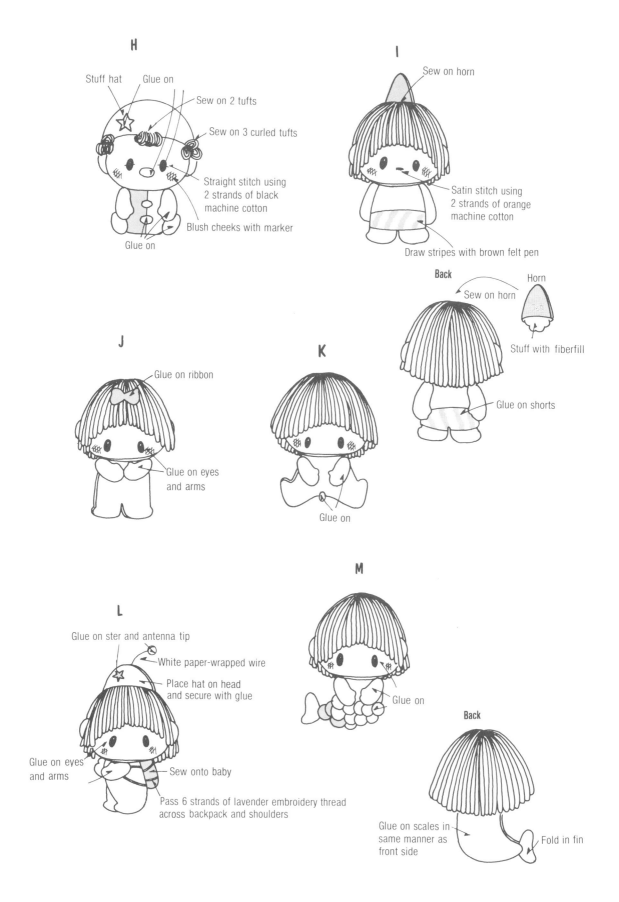

H

Stuff hat

Glue on

Sew on 2 tufts

Sew on 3 curled tufts

Straight stitch using
2 strands of black
machine cotton

Blush cheeks with marker

Glue on

I

Sew on horn

Satin stitch using
2 strands of orange
machine cotton

Draw stripes with brown felt pen

Back

Horn

Sew on horn

Stuff with fiberfill

Glue on shorts

J

Glue on ribbon

Glue on eyes
and arms

K

Glue on

L

Glue on ster and antenna tip

White paper-wrapped wire

Place hat on head
and secure with glue

Glue on eyes
and arms

Sew onto baby

Pass 6 strands of lavender embroidery thread
across backpack and shoulders

M

Glue on

Back

Glue on scales in
same manner as
front side

Fold in fin

Continued from pg. 6 *(CHOO CHOO TRAIN)*

Giraffe

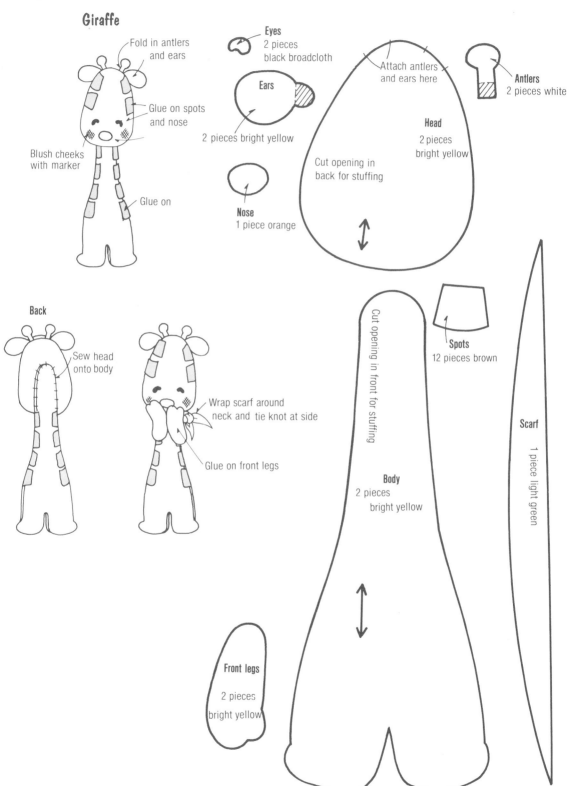

Fold in antlers and ears

Glue on spots and nose

Blush cheeks with marker

Glue on

Eyes
2 pieces
black broadcloth

Ears
2 pieces bright yellow

Nose
1 piece orange

Attach antlers and ears here

Head
2 pieces
bright yellow

Cut opening in back for stuffing

Antlers
2 pieces white

Spots
12 pieces brown

Cut opening in front for stuffing

Body
2 pieces
bright yellow

Scarf
1 piece light green

Back

Sew head onto body

Wrap scarf around neck and tie knot at side

Glue on front legs

Front legs
2 pieces
bright yellow

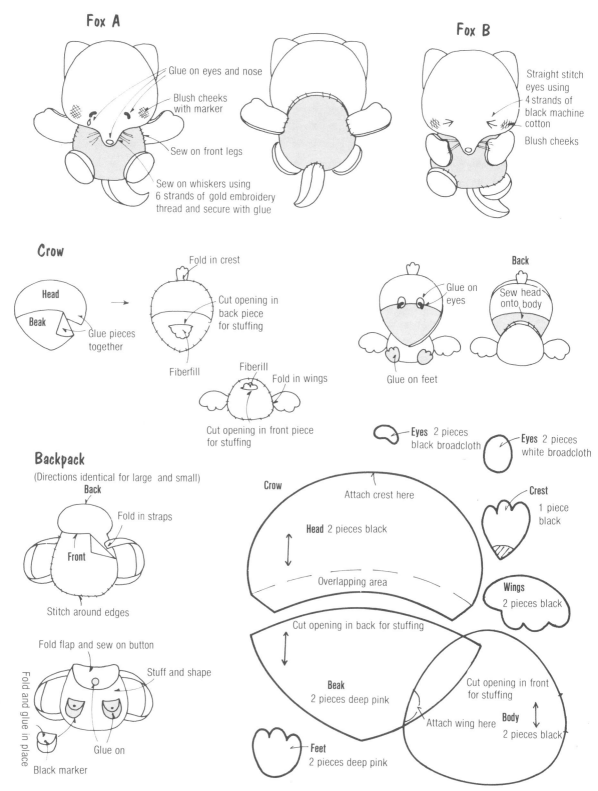

Fox A

Glue on eyes and nose

Blush cheeks with marker

Sew on front legs

Sew on whiskers using 6 strands of gold embroidery thread and secure with glue

Fox B

Straight stitch eyes using 4 strands of black machine cotton

Blush cheeks

Crow

Head

Beak

Glue pieces together

Fold in crest

Cut opening in back piece for stuffing

Fiberfill

Fiberill

Fold in wings

Cut opening in front piece for stuffing

Glue on eyes

Back

Sew head onto body

Glue on feet

Eyes 2 pieces black broadcloth

Eyes 2 pieces white broadcloth

Backpack

(Directions identical for large and small)

Back

Fold in straps

Front

Stitch around edges

Fold flap and sew on button

Stuff and shape

Fold and glue in place

Glue on

Black marker

Crow

Attach crest here

Head 2 pieces black

Overlapping area

Cut opening in back for stuffing

Beak 2 pieces deep pink

Feet 2 pieces deep pink

Cut opening in front for stuffing

Attach wing here

Body 2 pieces black

Crest 1 piece black

Wings 2 pieces black

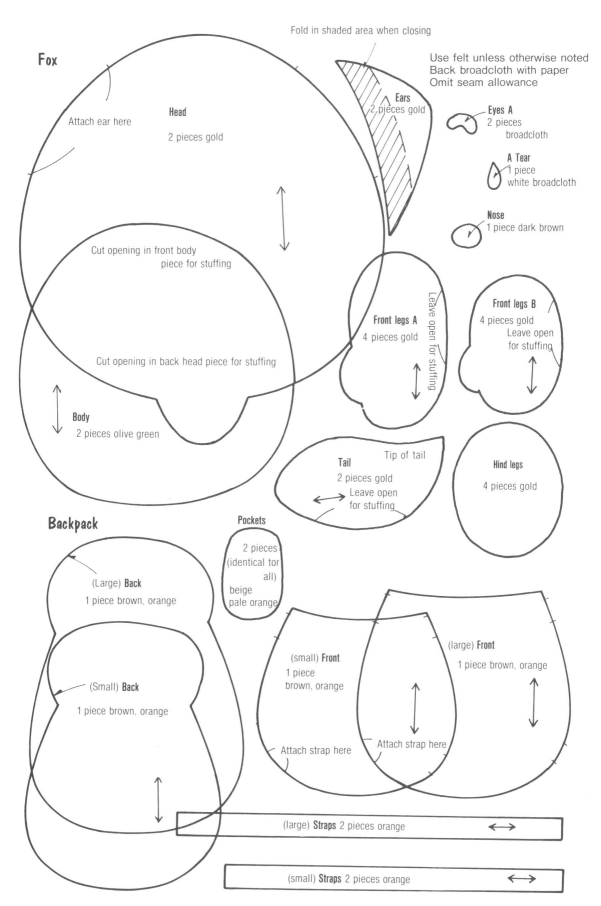

Fox

Fold in shaded area when closing

Use felt unless otherwise noted
Back broadcloth with paper
Omit seam allowance

Ears
2 pieces gold

Eyes A
2 pieces
broadcloth

A Tear
1 piece
white broadcloth

Nose
1 piece dark brown

Attach ear here

Head
2 pieces gold

Cut opening in front body
piece for stuffing

Front legs A
4 pieces gold

Leave open for stuffing

Front legs B
4 pieces gold
Leave open
for stuffing

Cut opening in back head piece for stuffing

Body
2 pieces olive green

Tail
2 pieces gold
Leave open
for stuffing

Tip of tail

Hind legs
4 pieces gold

Backpack

Pockets
2 pieces
(identical for
all)
beige
pale orange

(Large) **Back**
1 piece brown, orange

(Small) **Back**
1 piece brown, orange

(small) **Front**
1 piece
brown, orange

Attach strap here

(large) **Front**
1 piece brown, orange

Attach strap here

(large) **Straps** 2 pieces orange

(small) **Straps** 2 pieces orange

77

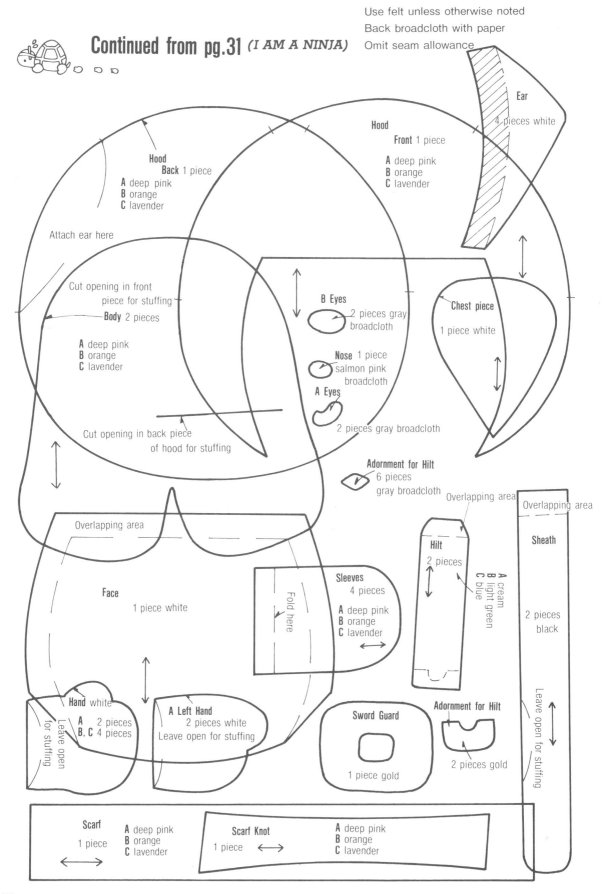

Continued from pg.31 *(I AM A NINJA)*

Use felt unless otherwise noted
Back broadcloth with paper
Omit seam allowance

Ear
4 pieces white

Hood
Back 1 piece
A deep pink
B orange
C lavender

Attach ear here

Hood
Front 1 piece
A deep pink
B orange
C lavender

Cut opening in front
piece for stuffing
Body 2 pieces
A deep pink
B orange
C lavender

Cut opening in back piece
of hood for stuffing

B Eyes
2 pieces gray
broadcloth

Nose 1 piece
salmon pink
broadcloth

A Eyes
2 pieces gray broadcloth

Chest piece
1 piece white

Adornment for Hilt
6 pieces
gray broadcloth

Overlapping area

Overlapping area

Overlapping area

Overlapping area

Hilt
2 pieces
A cream
B light green
C blue

Sheath
2 pieces
black

Leave open for stuffing

Face
1 piece white

Sleeves
4 pieces
A deep pink
B orange
C lavender

Fold here

Hand white
A   2 pieces
B, C 4 pieces
Leave open for stuffing

A Left Hand
2 pieces white
Leave open for stuffing

Sword Guard
1 piece gold

Adornment for Hilt
2 pieces gold

Scarf
1 piece
A deep pink
B orange
C lavender

Scarf Knot
1 piece
A deep pink
B orange
C lavender

78

Continued from pg.35 *(FRIENDLY ANIMALS)*

Patterns for FRIENDLY ANIMALS on pg. 93

Zebra

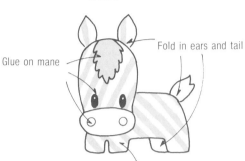

Glue on mane

Fold in ears and tail

Draw strips with gray felt pen

Tiger

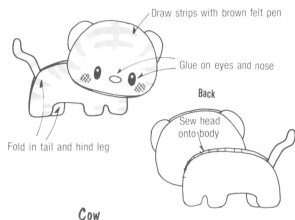

Draw strips with brown felt pen

Glue on eyes and nose

Fold in tail and hind leg

Back

Sew head onto body

Lion

Fold in ears

Glue on eyes and nose

Back

Fold in tail and hind leg

Glue on mane

Sew head onto body

Glue on tip of tail

Cow

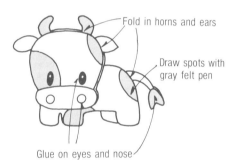

Fold in horns and ears

Draw spots with gray felt pen

Glue on eyes and nose

Koala Bear

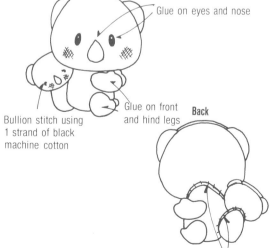

Glue on eyes and nose

Glue on front and hind legs

Back

Bullion stitch using 1 strand of black machine cotton

Sew head and baby bear onto body

Hippopotamus

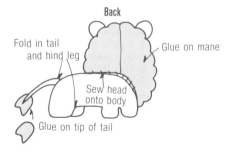

Fold in ears, tail and hind leg

Glue on eyes and nostrils

Continued from pg.43 *(QUARTET)*

☆ ☆ ☆

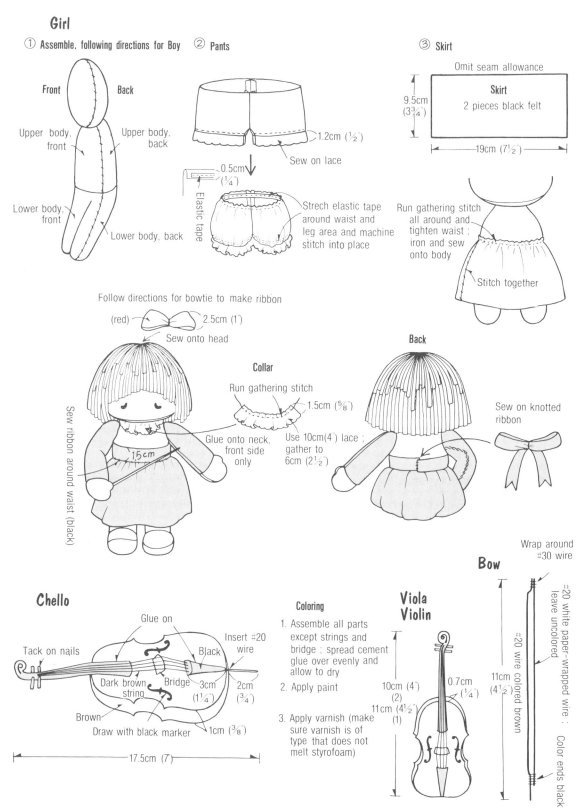

Girl

① Assemble, following directions for Boy

Front   **Back**

Upper body, front

Upper body, back

Lower body, front

Lower body, back

② Pants

1.2cm (½")

Sew on lace

0.5cm (¼")

Elastic tape

Strech elastic tape around waist and leg area and machine stitch into place

③ Skirt

Omit seam allowance

Skirt
2 pieces black felt

9.5cm (3¾")

19cm (7½")

Run gathering stitch all around and tighten waist ; iron and sew onto body

Stitch together

Follow directions for bowtie to make ribbon

(red)   2.5cm (1")

Sew onto head

Sew ribbon around waist (black)

1.5 cm

Collar

Run gathering stitch

1.5cm (⅝")

Glue onto neck, front side only

Use 10cm(4") lace ; gather to 6cm (2½")

Back

Sew on knotted ribbon

Chello

Glue on

Tack on nails

Dark brown string

Bridge

Brown

Black

Insert #20 wire

3cm (1¼")

2cm (¾")

Draw with black marker

1cm (⅜")

17.5cm (7")

Coloring

1. Assemble all parts except strings and bridge ; spread cement glue over evenly and allow to dry

2. Apply paint

3. Apply varnish (make sure varnish is of type that does not melt styrofoam)

Viola Violin

10cm (4") (2)

11cm (4½") (1)

0.7cm (¼")

Bow

Wrap around #30 wire

#20 white paper-wrapped wire ; leave uncolored

#20 wire colored brown

Color ends black

11cm (4½")

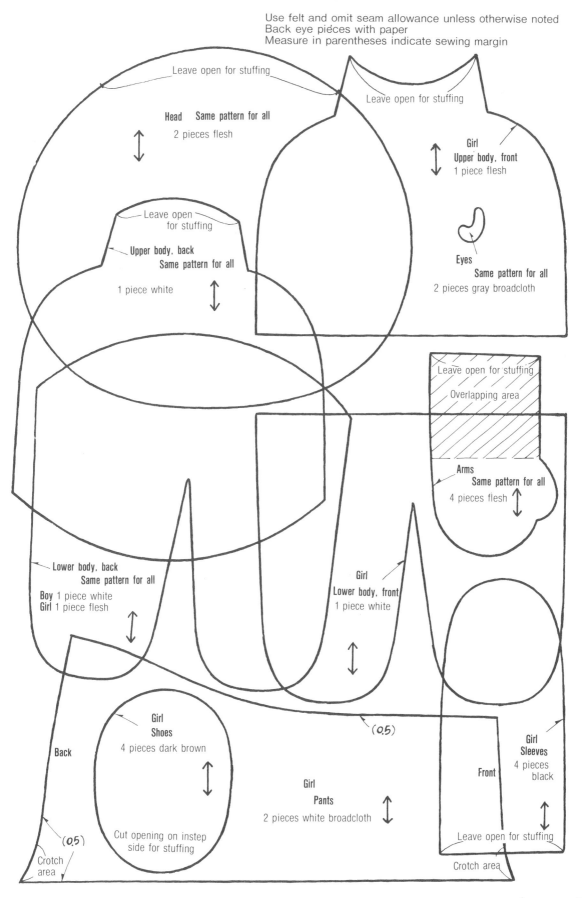

Use felt and omit seam allowance unless otherwise noted
Back eye pieces with paper
Measure in parentheses indicate sewing margin

Leave open for stuffing

Leave open for stuffing

Head   Same pattern for all
2 pieces flesh

Girl
Upper body, front
1 piece flesh

Leave open
for stuffing

Upper body, back
Same pattern for all

1 piece white

Eyes
Same pattern for all
2 pieces gray broadcloth

Leave open for stuffing

Overlapping area

Arms
Same pattern for all
4 pieces flesh

Lower body, back
Same pattern for all

Boy 1 piece white
Girl 1 piece flesh

Girl
Lower body, front
1 piece white

Girl
Shoes
4 pieces dark brown

Back

(0.5)

Girl
Pants
2 pieces white broadcloth

Front

Girl
Sleeves
4 pieces
black

Leave open for stuffing

(0.5)

Crotch
area

Cut opening on instep
side for stuffing

Crotch area

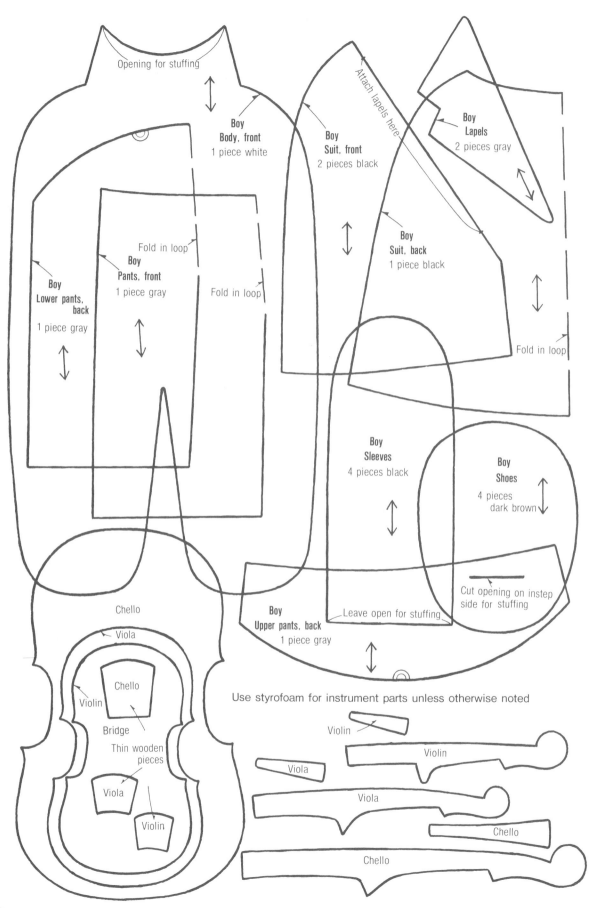

Opening for stuffing

Boy
Body, front
1 piece white

Boy
Suit, front
2 pieces black

Attach lapels here

Boy
Lapels
2 pieces gray

Boy
Suit, back
1 piece black

Fold in loop

Boy
Pants, front
1 piece gray

Fold in loop

Boy
Lower pants, back
1 piece gray

Fold in loop

Boy
Sleeves
4 pieces black

Boy
Shoes
4 pieces dark brown

Cut opening on instep side for stuffing

Chello

Viola

Violin

Chello

Bridge

Thin wooden pieces

Viola

Violin

Boy
Upper pants, back
1 piece gray

Leave open for stuffing

Use styrofoam for instrument parts unless otherwise noted

Violin

Violin

Viola

Viola

Chello

Chello

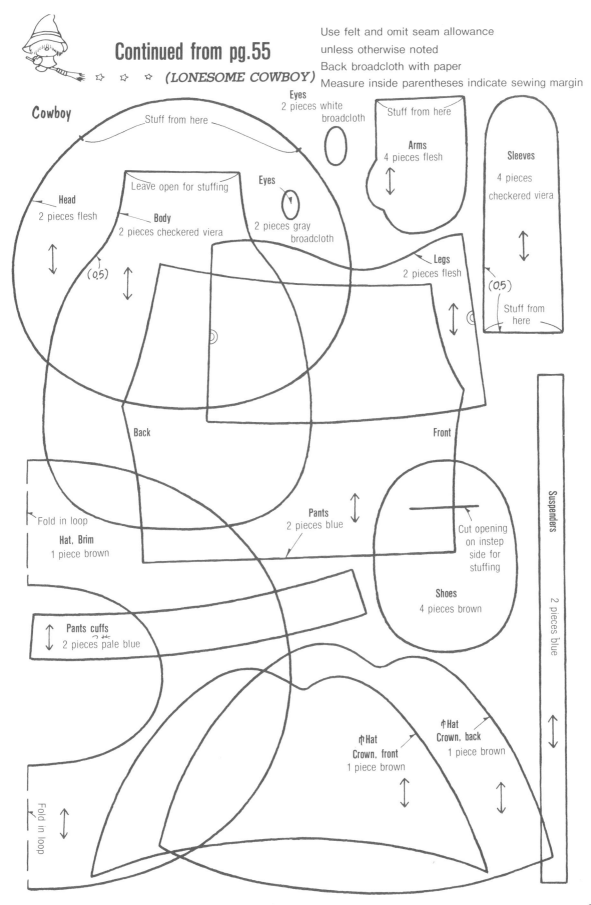

Continued from pg.55

(LONESOME COWBOY)

☆ ☆ ☆

Use felt and omit seam allowance
unless otherwise noted
Back broadcloth with paper
Measure inside parentheses indicate sewing margin

Cowboy

Stuff from here

Eyes
2 pieces white
broadcloth

Stuff from here

Arms
4 pieces flesh

Sleeves

4 pieces
checkered viera

Head
2 pieces flesh

Leave open for stuffing

Body
2 pieces checkered viera

Eyes

2 pieces gray
broadcloth

Legs
2 pieces flesh

(0.5)

(0.5)

Stuff from
here

Back

Front

Fold in loop

Hat, Brim
1 piece brown

Pants
2 pieces blue

Cut opening
on instep
side for
stuffing

Shoes
4 pieces brown

Suspenders

2 pieces blue

Pants cuffs
2 pieces pale blue

Fold in loop

中Hat
Crown, front
1 piece brown

中Hat
Crown, back
1 piece brown

Frog

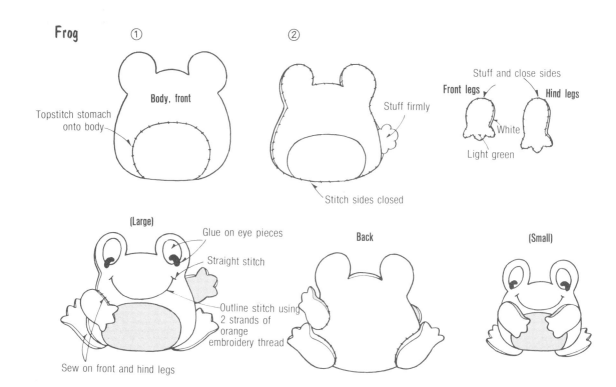

① Body, front

Topstitch stomach onto body

② Stuff firmly

Stitch sides closed

Front legs — Stuff and close sides — Hind legs

White

Light green

(Large)

Glue on eye pieces

Straight stitch

Outline stitch using 2 strands of orange embroidery thread

Sew on front and hind legs

Back

(Small)

Horse

Ears

Outer ear

Glue pieces together

Inner ear

Head

Topstitch

Muzzle area

Glue pieces together

Back

Fold in ears

Stuff firmly from opening in back

Stitch sides closed

Body

Stuff firmly from opening in front

Fold in tail

Stitch sides closed

Glue on hoofs and topstitch to secure in place

Tie string around neck

Glue on mane

Glue on eyes and nostrils

Blush cheeks with marker

Sew on hind leg

Hind leg

Attach hoof

Stuff and close sides

Tail

Do not stuff at root

Back

Sew on head and right hind leg to body

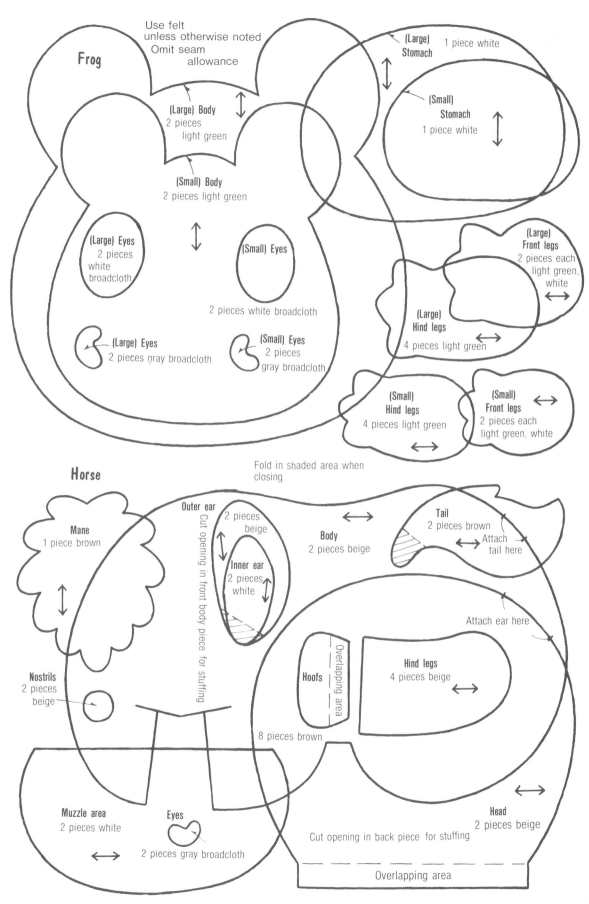

Frog

Use felt
unless otherwise noted
Omit seam
allowance

(Large) Body
2 pieces
light green

(Small) Body
2 pieces light green

(Large) Eyes
2 pieces
white
broadcloth

(Small) Eyes

2 pieces white broadcloth

(Large) Eyes
2 pieces gray broadcloth

(Small) Eyes
2 pieces
gray broadcloth

(Large)
Stomach   1 piece white

(Small)
Stomach
1 piece white

(Large)
Front legs
2 pieces each
light green,
white

(Large)
Hind legs
4 pieces light green

(Small)
Hind legs
4 pieces light green

(Small)
Front legs
2 pieces each
light green, white

Horse

Fold in shaded area when
closing

Mane
1 piece brown

Outer ear
2 pieces
beige

Inner ear
2 pieces
white

Cut opening in front body piece for stuffing

Body
2 pieces beige

Tail
2 pieces brown

Attach
tail here

Attach ear here

Nostrils
2 pieces
beige

Hoofs

Overlapping area

Hind legs
4 pieces beige

8 pieces brown

Muzzle area
2 pieces white

Eyes

2 pieces gray broadcloth

Head
2 pieces beige

Cut opening in back piece for stuffing

Overlapping area

85

Continued from pg.47 *(FOOTBALL)*

☆ ☆ ☆

Use felt unless otherwise noted
Omit seam allowance

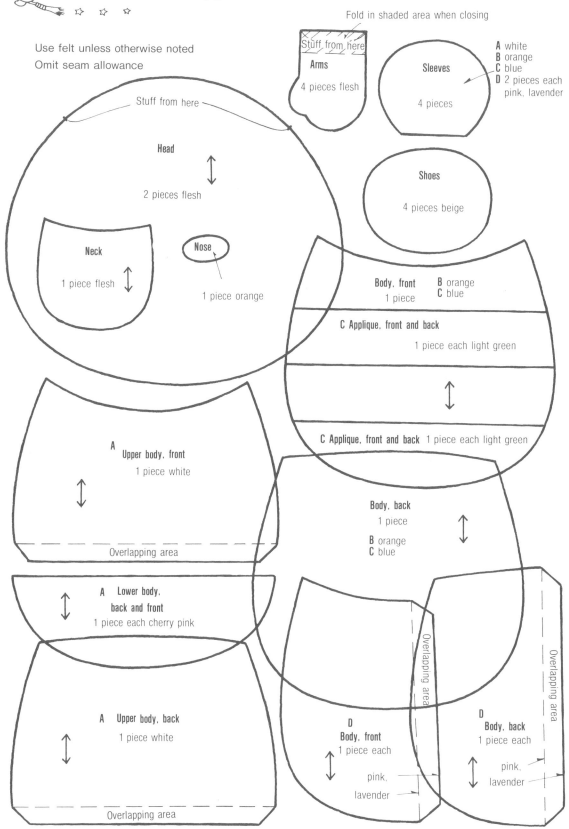

Fold in shaded area when closing

Stuff from here

Arms

4 pieces flesh

Sleeves

4 pieces

A white
B orange
C blue
D 2 pieces each pink, lavender

Stuff from here

Head

2 pieces flesh

Shoes

4 pieces beige

Neck

1 piece flesh

Nose

1 piece orange

Body, front
1 piece

B orange
C blue

C Applique, front and back

1 piece each light green

C Applique, front and back 1 piece each light green

A
Upper body, front
1 piece white

Body, back
1 piece

B orange
C blue

Overlapping area

A   **Lower body,**
back and front
1 piece each cherry pink

Overlapping area

Overlapping area

A   **Upper body, back**
1 piece white

D
Body, front
1 piece each

pink,

lavender

D
Body, back
1 piece each

pink,
lavender

Overlapping area

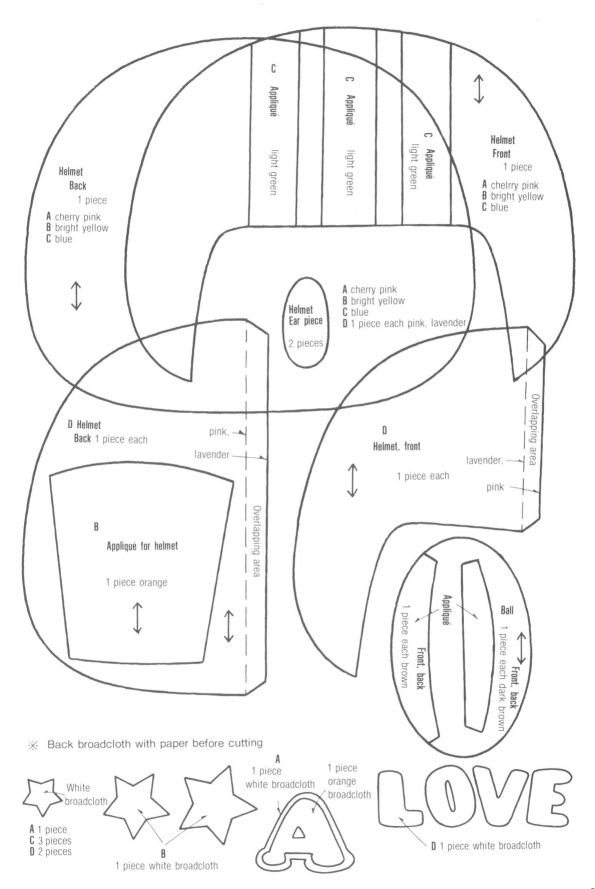

C
Appliqué
light green

C
Appliqué
light green

C
Appliqué
light green

Helmet
Front
1 piece

A chelrry pink
B bright yellow
C blue

Helmet
Back
1 piece

A cherry pink
B bright yellow
C blue

Helmet
Ear piece

2 pieces

A cherry pink
B bright yellow
C blue
D 1 piece each pink, lavender

pink,

lavender

D Helmet
Back 1 piece each

Overlapping area

D
Helmet, front

1 piece each

lavender,

pink

Overlapping area

B

Appliqué for helmet

1 piece orange

Appliqué
Front, back
1 piece each brown

Ball

Front, back
1 piece each dark brown

※ Back broadcloth with paper before cutting

White
broadcloth

A 1 piece
C 3 pieces
D 2 pieces

B
1 piece white broadcloth

A
1 piece
white broadcloth

1 piece
orange
broadcloth

LOVE

D 1 piece white broadcloth

Continued from pg.59 *(SUMMER VACATION)*

① **Skirt** (Measures include sewing margin)

4cm
(1½")

↕ 1 piece white broadcloth

←———— 19.5cm(7¾") ————→

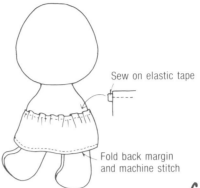

Sew on elastic tape

Fold back margin
and machine stitch

② **T shirt**

Wrap sleeves and neckline
with white vias tape

Fold back margin and machine stitch

③ **Pochette Bag**

Fold flap

6 strands of white
embroidery thread,
approx. 20cm(8") in length

Glue flap in place

Glue thread in place under flap

Sew on bead

C

Glue on eyes and nose

Make bowtie knots
and glue on ribbons

Draw freckles

Blush cheeks

Sew Arm onto T shirt

Hang pochette bag
over sholders

Necessary Materials for Making Dolls

Tailoring Shears Used for cutting fabric and trimming hair. In addition, smaller shears may be useful for cutting tiny pieces (eyes, nose, etc.).

Paper Shears Used for cutting out paper patterns.

Screw Driver Used for stuffing dolls. Longer ones, such as those used for adjusting radios, are easier to work with.

Pencil Use 2B for transferring patterns to fabric, and white colored pencils on darker fabrics.

Pins Used for securing fabrics in place. Also helpful in determining position of eyes, arms, etc.

Sewing Needle Sharps   #s 9 through 11 are best for making dolls.

Machine Needle Use #11 needle.

Cement Glue Used for crafts and woodworks.

Cotton Swabs Used for applying glue.

Others Iron, hair blower.

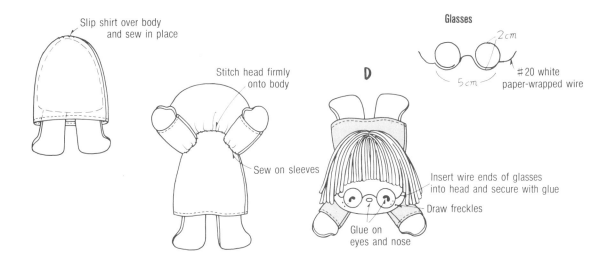

Slip shirt over body
and sew in place

Stitch head firmly
onto body

Sew on sleeves

Glasses

2cm

5cm

#20 white
paper-wrapped wire

D

Insert wire ends of glasses
into head and secure with glue

Draw freckles

Glue on
eyes and nose

Omit seam allowance unless other wise noted
Back eyes, nose, pockets and buttons with paper
Measure inside parentheses indicate sewing margin

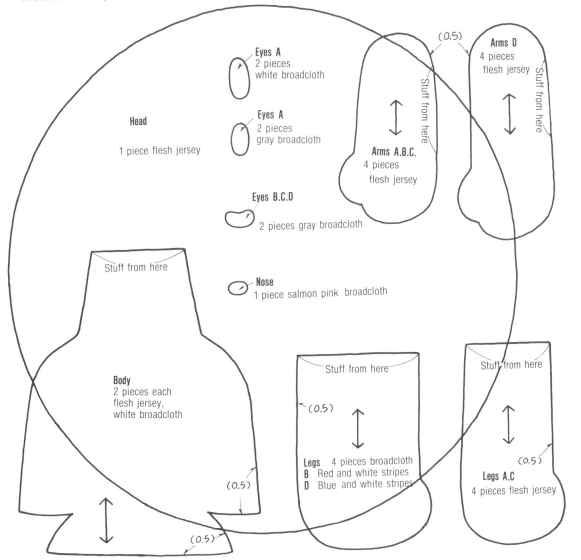

Head

1 piece flesh jersey

Eyes A
2 pieces
white broadcloth

Eyes A
2 pieces
gray broadcloth

Eyes B.C.D

2 pieces gray broadcloth

Nose
1 piece salmon pink broadcloth

Arms A.B.C.
4 pieces
flesh jersey

Stuff from here

(0.5)

Arms D
4 pieces
flesh jersey

Stuff from here

Stuff from here

Body
2 pieces each
flesh jersey,
white broadcloth

Stuff from here

(0.5)

(0.5)

Stuff from here

(0.5)

Legs   4 pieces broadcloth
B   Red and white stripes
D   Blue and white stripes

Stuff from here

(0.5)

Legs A.C
4 pieces flesh jersey

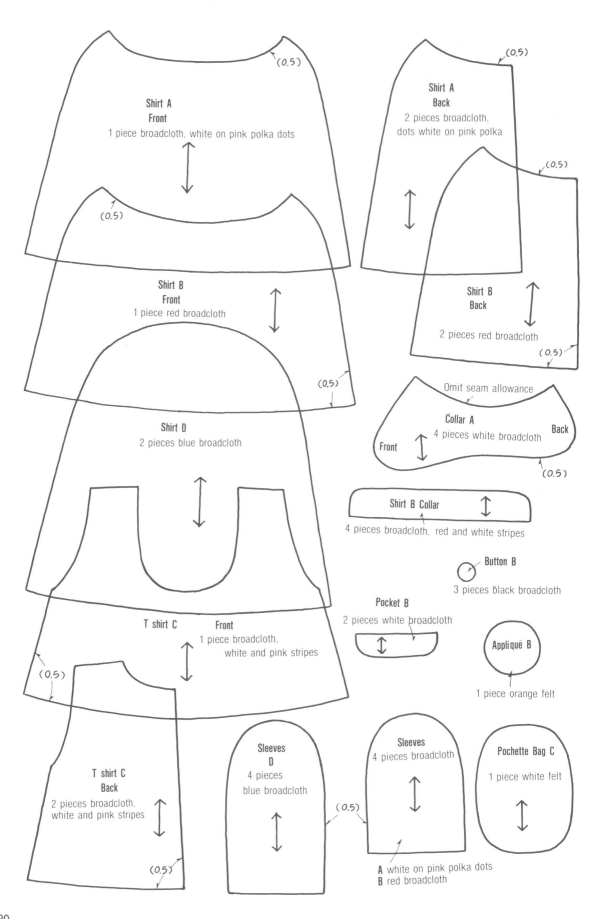

Shirt A
Front
1 piece broadcloth, white on pink polka dots

(0.5)

Shirt A
Back
2 pieces broadcloth,
dots white on pink polka

(0.5)

(0.5)

Shirt B
Front
1 piece red broadcloth

Shirt B
Back

2 pieces red broadcloth

(0.5)

(0.5)

Shirt D
2 pieces blue broadcloth

(0.5)

Omit seam allowance

Collar A
4 pieces white broadcloth

Front

Back

(0.5)

Shirt B Collar

4 pieces broadcloth, red and white stripes

Button B

3 pieces black broadcloth

T shirt C   Front
1 piece broadcloth,
white and pink stripes

Pocket B

2 pieces white broadcloth

Appliqué B

1 piece orange felt

(0.5)

T shirt C
Back

2 pieces broadcloth,
white and pink stripes

(0.5)

Sleeves
D
4 pieces
blue broadcloth

Sleeves
4 pieces broadcloth

Pochette Bag C

1 piece white felt

(0.5)

A white on pink polka dots
B red broadcloth

Continued from pg.63 *(HAPPY WEDDING)*

☆ ☆ ☆

Sleeping Boy

① Head, Body

Head

Stitch sides closed

Body

Stuffing

Stuffing

→

Stitch sides closed

Glue overlapping area and attach shoes to pants

②

Sew on head

③ Hair

Make 63 tufts of curls

Tip of marker

1cm (3/8")

Wrap around 12 times

→

Tie at end, using same yarn

Sew on tufts all over head

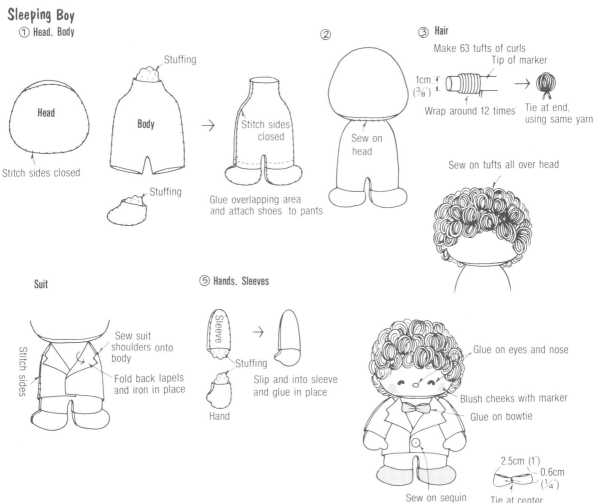

Suit

Stitch sides

Sew suit shoulders onto body

Fold back lapels and iron in place

⑤ Hands, Sleeves

Sleeve

Stuffing

Hand

→

Slip and into sleeve and glue in place

Glue on eyes and nose

Blush cheeks with marker

Glue on bowtie

Sew on sequin

2.5cm (1")

0.6cm (1/4")

Tie at center

Bride

※ Assemble body following directions for Sleeping Boy

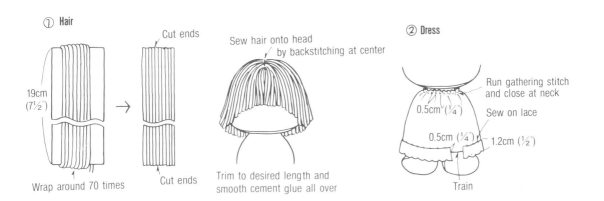

① Hair

19cm (7½")

Wrap around 70 times

Cut ends

→

Cut ends

Cut ends

Sew hair onto head by backstitching at center

Trim to desired length and smooth cement glue all over

② Dress

Run gathering stitch and close at neck

0.5cm (¼")

Sew on lace

0.5cm (¼")

1.2cm (½")

Train

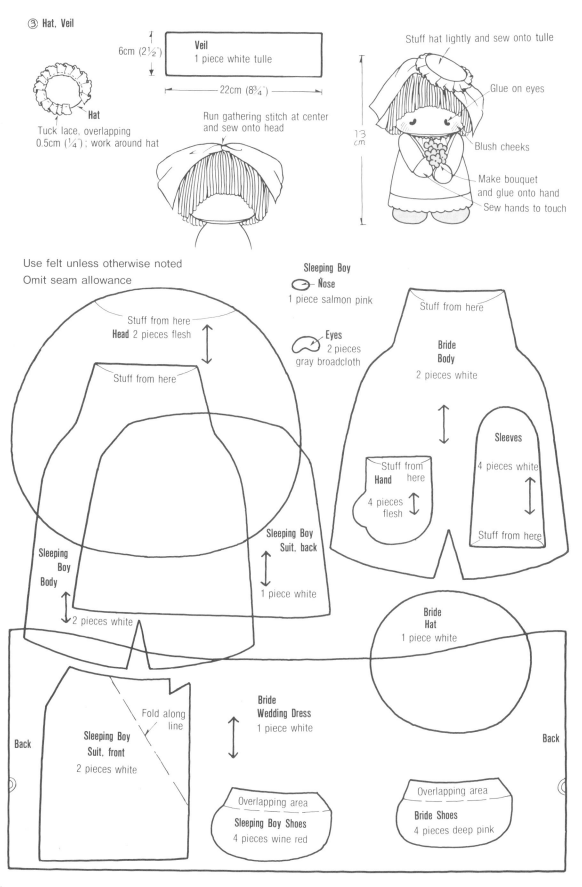

③ Hat, Veil

6cm (2½")

Veil
1 piece white tulle

22cm (8¾")

Run gathering stitch at center
and sew onto head

Hat

Tuck lace, overlapping
0.5cm (¼"); work around hat

Stuff hat lightly and sew onto tulle

Glue on eyes

Blush cheeks

Make bouquet
and glue onto hand

Sew hands to touch

13 cm

Use felt unless otherwise noted
Omit seam allowance

Sleeping Boy

Nose
1 piece salmon pink

Eyes
2 pieces
gray broadcloth

Stuff from here
Head 2 pieces flesh

Stuff from here

Stuff from here

Bride
Body
2 pieces white

Sleeves
4 pieces white

Stuff from here
Hand
4 pieces flesh

Stuff from here

Sleeping
Boy
Body

2 pieces white

Sleeping Boy
Suit, back

1 piece white

Bride
Hat
1 piece white

Back

Fold along line

Sleeping Boy
Suit, front

2 pieces white

Bride
Wedding Dress
1 piece white

Back

Overlapping area

Sleeping Boy Shoes
4 pieces wine red

Overlapping area

Bride Shoes
4 pieces deep pink

ACTUAL SIZE PATTERNS
(FRIENDLY ANIMALS, WELCOME TO FANTASY LAND)

♥ *Glue patterns to cardboard or firm paper before cutting.*
♥ *Omit seam allowance for all patterns in insert.*
♥ *Cut opening for stuffing on side that becomes hidden when assembled.*
♥ *Apply cement glue where "overlapping" is indicated.*
♥ *Fold in shaded area when stitching pieces together.*
♥ *Where broadcloth is indicated, back with paper before assembling.*
   Use felt otherwise.

RABBIT

Attach ears here

Head
2 pieces white

Cut opening (1 piece only)

Cut opening (1 piece only)

Body
2 pieces white

Ears
2 pieces white

Hind legs
2 pieces white

Front legs
2 pieces white

Eyes
2 pieces
black broadcloth

Nose
1 piece
salmon pink
broadcloth

ZEBRA

Head
2 pieces white

Overlapping area

Body
2 pieces white

Attach tail here

Hind leg
1 piece white

Muzzle area
2 pieces pale orange

2 pieces white

Mane
1 piece
gray

1 piece gray

Tail

Ears

Eyes
2 pieces
black broadcloth

Nostrils
2 pieces
gray broadcloth

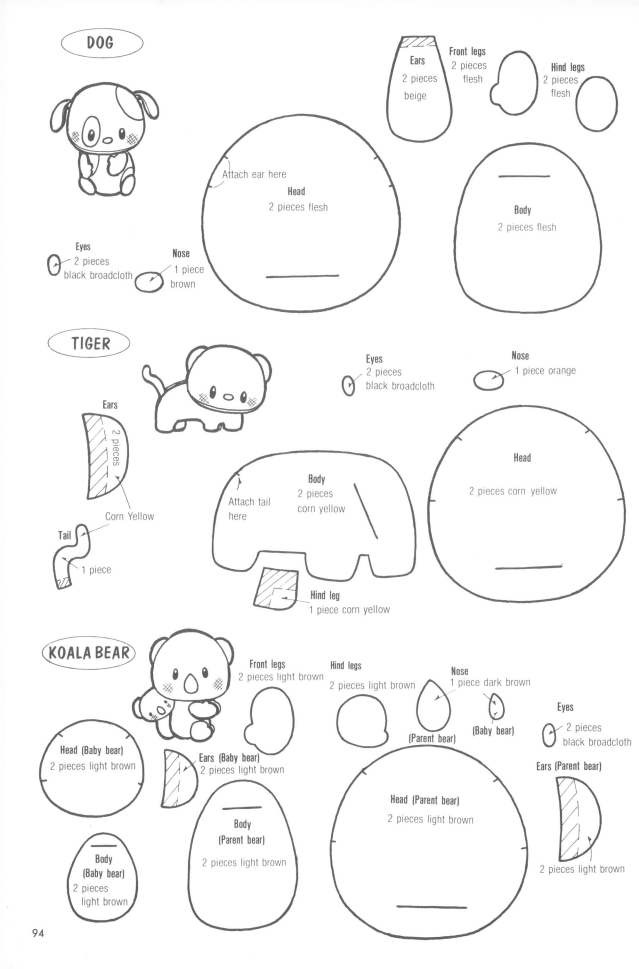

DOG

Ears
2 pieces
beige

Front legs
2 pieces
flesh

Hind legs
2 pieces
flesh

Head
2 pieces flesh

Attach ear here

Body
2 pieces flesh

Eyes
2 pieces
black broadcloth

Nose
1 piece
brown

TIGER

Ears
2 pieces
Corn Yellow

Eyes
2 pieces
black broadcloth

Nose
1 piece orange

Tail
1 piece

Body
2 pieces
corn yellow

Attach tail
here

Head
2 pieces corn yellow

Hind leg
1 piece corn yellow

KOALA BEAR

Front legs
2 pieces light brown

Hind legs
2 pieces light brown

Nose
1 piece dark brown

(Parent bear)

(Baby bear)

Eyes
2 pieces
black broadcloth

Head (Baby bear)
2 pieces light brown

Ears (Baby bear)
2 pieces light brown

Head (Parent bear)
2 pieces light brown

Ears (Parent bear)
2 pieces light brown

Body
(Parent bear)
2 pieces light brown

Body
(Baby bear)
2 pieces
light brown

COW

Horns
2 pieces gray

Tail
1 piece white

Attach horn here

Attach ear here

Head
2 pieces white

Ears
2 pieces white

Tip of tail
2 pieces gray

Body
2 pieces white

Attach tail here

Eyes
2 pieces
black broadcloth

Overlapping area

Nostrils
2 pieces
gray broadcloth

Muzzle area
2 pieces flesh

Hind leg
1 piece white

LION

Eyes
2 pieces
black broadcloth

Ears
2 pieces white

Nose
1 piece
pale orange

Tail
1 piece white

Head
2 pieces white

Top

Mane
2 pieces gray

Bottom

Body
2 pieces white

Attach tail here

Tip of tail
2 pieces gray

Hind leg
1 piece white

MOUSE

Eyes
2 pieces
black broadcloth

Front legs
2 pieces cream

MOLE

Eyes
1 piece
black broadcloth

Ears
2 pieces
cream

Body
2 pieces deep pink

Head
2 pieces cream

Body
2 pieces cream

Legs
4 pieces deep pink

Stuff from here

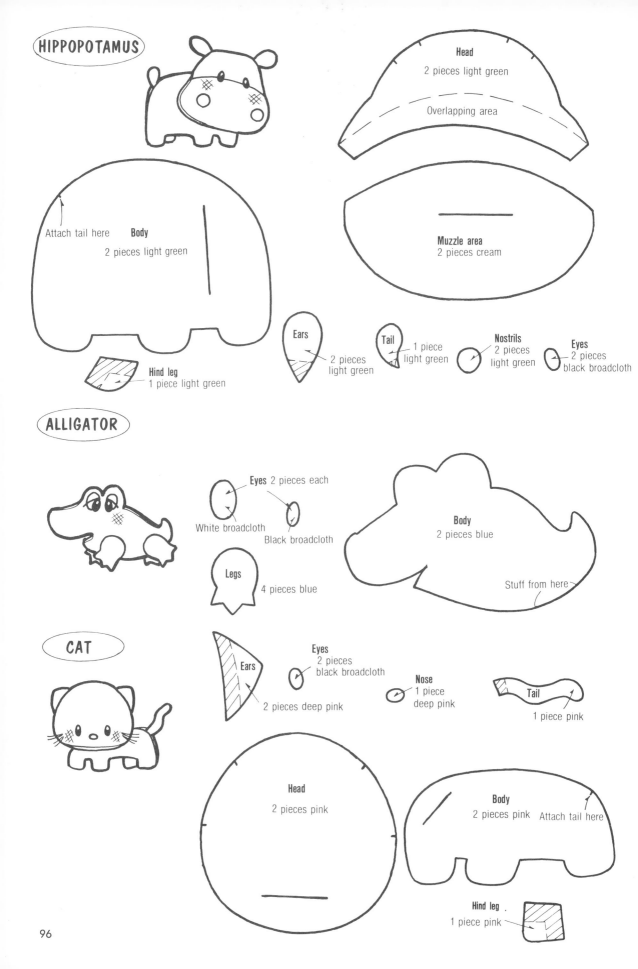

HIPPOPOTAMUS

Head
2 pieces light green

Overlapping area

Attach tail here   **Body**
2 pieces light green

Muzzle area
2 pieces cream

Ears
2 pieces
light green

Tail
1 piece
light green

Nostrils
2 pieces
light green

Eyes
2 pieces
black broadcloth

Hind leg
1 piece light green

ALLIGATOR

Eyes 2 pieces each

White broadcloth

Black broadcloth

Body
2 pieces blue

Stuff from here

Legs
4 pieces blue

CAT

Ears
2 pieces deep pink

Eyes
2 pieces
black broadcloth

Nose
1 piece
deep pink

Tail
1 piece pink

Head
2 pieces pink

Body
2 pieces pink   Attach tail here

Hind leg
1 piece pink

PANDA BEAR

Tail
1 piece gray

Eyes
2 pieces black broadcloth

Eye area
2 pieces
gray

Ears
2 pieces gray

Nose
1 piece salmon pink broadcloth

Legs
4 pieces
gray

Head
2 pieces white

Attach tail here

Body
2 pieces white

WolF

1 piece brown

1 piece brown

Ears

Tail

Attach tail here   Body
2 pieces brown

Head
2 pieces brown

Tongue

1 piece orange

Eye
1 piece black broadcloth

Hind leg
1 piece brown

LEOPARD

Eyes
2 pieces black broadcloth

Front legs

Nose
1 piece deep pink

2 pieces pale orange

Head
2 pieces pale orange

Ears

Hind legs
2 pieces

2 pieces   Pale orange

Tail 1 piece

Body
2 pieces pale orange

Attach tail here

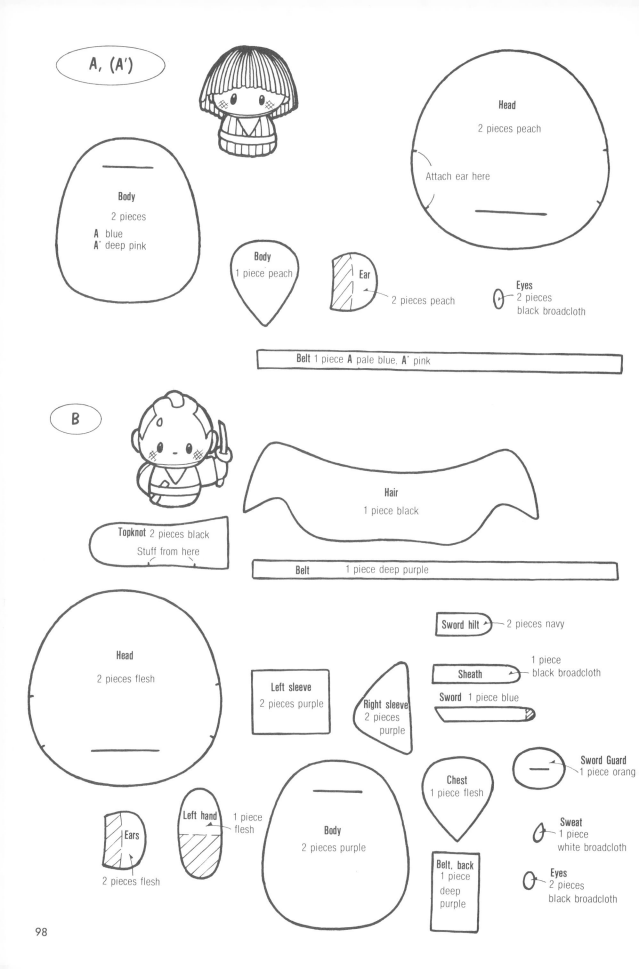

A, (A')

Head
2 pieces peach

Attach ear here

Body
2 pieces
A blue
A' deep pink

Body
1 piece peach

Ear
2 pieces peach

Eyes
2 pieces
black broadcloth

Belt 1 piece **A** pale blue, **A'** pink

B

Hair
1 piece black

Topknot 2 pieces black
Stuff from here

Belt   1 piece deep purple

Sword hilt — 2 pieces navy

Sheath — 1 piece
black broadcloth

Sword 1 piece blue

Head
2 pieces flesh

Left sleeve
2 pieces purple

Right sleeve
2 pieces
purple

Sword Guard
1 piece orang

Chest
1 piece flesh

Sweat
1 piece
white broadcloth

Left hand | 1 piece
flesh

Body
2 pieces purple

Ears
2 pieces flesh

Belt, back
1 piece
deep
purple

Eyes
2 pieces
black broadcloth

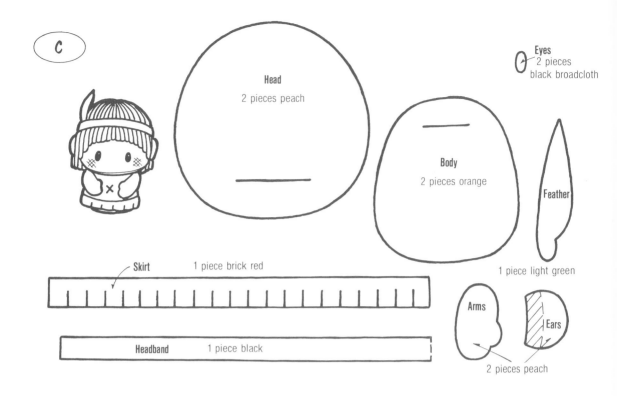

C

Head
2 pieces peach

Body
2 pieces orange

Eyes
2 pieces
black broadcloth

Feather
1 piece light green

Skirt   1 piece brick red

Headband   1 piece black

Arms

Ears

2 pieces peach

D

E

Vest
1 piece black

Body

2 pieces

D gray
E brown

Head
2 pieces flesh

Chest
1 piece flesh

Ears

2 pieces
flesh

Arms

2 pieces
flesh

Eyes
2 pieces
black broadcloth

Belt 1 piece D dark gray, E dark brown

F

Ears
2 pieces flesh

Head
2 pieces flesh

Right arm
1 piece flesh

Left arm
1 piece flesh

Feet
2 pieces dark brown

Hat, back
1 piece dark brown

Body
2 pieces mustard yellow

Rolled mat
1 piece beige

Patch on hat
1 piece mustard yellow

Hat, front
1 piece dark brown

Eyes
2 pieces black broadcloth

G

Head
2 pieces flesh

Ears
2 pieces flesh

Arms
2 pieces flesh

Feet
2 pieces flesh

Pompon
2 pieces white

Upper part of hat
1 piece light green

Body, right
2 pieces blue

Overlapping area

Body, left
2 pieces light green

Hat, right
2 pieces blue

Overlapping area

Hat, left
2 pieces light green

Eyes
2 pieces black broadcloth

H

Head
2 pieces peach

Eyes
2 pieces
black broadcloth

Nose
1 piece orange

Button
2 pieces white

Hat, back
1 piece dark brown

Hat, front
1 piece dark brown

Body, right
2 pieces
lavender

Overlapping area

Body, left
2 pieces
deep pink

Ears
2 pieces
peach

Appliqué
1 piece
orange bloadcloth

Arms

Legs

2 pieces peach

I

Head
2 pieces flesh

Body
2 pieces flesh

Horn
2 pieces
orange
Stuff from
here

Ears
2 pieces flesh

Eyes
2 pieces
black broadcloth

Arms
2 pieces
flesh

Shorts
2 pieces mustard yellow

J

Body
2 pieces flesh

Ribbon
1 piece pink

Arms
2 pieces
flesh

Eyes
2 pieces
black broadcloth

Head
2 pieces flesh

Ears
2 pieces flesh

101

K

Ears
2 pieces flesh

Eyes
2 pieces
black broadcloth

Head
2 pieces flesh

Arms
2 pieces
flesh

Peanut
1 piece flesh

Body
2 pieces flesh

M

Scales
20 pieces pink
6 pieces deep pink

Eyes
2 pieces
black broadcloth

Ears
2 pieces
flesh

Arms
2 pieces
flesh

Head
2 pieces flesh

Body
2 pieces flesh

Fin
1 piece white

L

Head
2 pieces peach

Arms
2 pieces
peach

Eyes
2 pieces
black broadcloth

Ears
2 pieces peach

Body
2 pieces gray

Pompon
2 pieces gray

Appliqué
1 piece
white broadcloth

Oxygen Tank
2 pieces
blue
Stuff from
here

Right leg
2 pieces gray

Hat
2 pieces gray